W9-DFT-280

2011

TRENDSPOTTING
FOR THE
NEXT DECADE

LAERMERABILIA

Other Books by Laermer

Native's Guide to New York (1989, 1991, 1995, 1998, 2002)

Bargain Hunting in Greater New York (1990)

Get On With It (1997)

TrendSpotting (2002); also e-book

Full Frontal PR (2003, 2004); also e-book

Punk Marketing—coauthored by Mark Simmons (2007); also
e-book and audio via audible.com/punkmarketing.com

Coming soon . . . Full Frontal PR 2: When PR Ruled the World

Laermer Blog Destinations

Laermer.com/blog

unspunradio.com

badpitch.blogspot.com

Laermer Site

Unstoppable Laermer.com

Contact Laermer

E-mail: richard@Laermer.com
        and

Snail-mail thank-you notes, critiques, job offers, proposals,
nonserious threats:

Richard Laermer

PMB 269

49–950 Jefferson Street

Indio, CA 92201

Newsletter Hook-Up

nosnoozeletter@Laermer.com

2011

TRENDSPOTTING
FOR THE
NEXT DECADE

RICHARD LAERMER

McGraw Hill

New York | Chicago | San Francisco
Lisbon | London | Madrid | Mexico City | Milan
New Delhi | San Juan | Seoul | Singapore
Sydney | Toronto

The **McGraw·Hill** Companies

Copyright ©2008 by Richard Laermer. All rights reserved. Printed in the United States of America. Except as permitted under the United States Copyright Act of 1976, no part of this publication may be reproduced or distributed in any form or by any means, or stored in a data base or retrieval system, without the prior written permission of the publisher.

1 2 3 4 5 6 7 8 9 0   DOC/DOC   0 9 8

ISBN   978-0-07-149727-5
MHID   0-07-149727-7

McGraw-Hill books are available at special quantity discounts to use as premiums and sales promotions, or for use in corporate training programs. To contact a representative please visit the Contact Us pages at www.mhprofessional.com.

Library of Congress Cataloging-in-Publication Data

Laermer, Richard
  2011 : trendspotting for the next decade / Richard Laermer.
    p. cm.
  Includes index.
  ISBN 978-0-07-149727-5 (alk. paper)
  1. Twenty-first century—Forecasts. 2. Social prediction. 3. Technological forecasting. I. Title.
  CB161.L33 2008
  303.4909'0512—dc22

                                                    2008008333

This book is printed on acid-free paper.

I wrote the crux of this on one of a bunch of new-model BlackBerries, so I am guessing this is it:

Not possible without the able assistance of Research in Motion.

I'm open to sponsorship. As the world's fastest thumb typist, I'm a freaking athlete; think about it.

The future of the book is the blurb.

—Marshall McLuhan

*Don't worry head. The computer will do
all the thinking from now on.*

—Homer Simpson

Contents

Intro

Induction into 2011

Welcome to a business book for the next decade.

Nice slogan, eh? Anyway, yes, uh-huh, you can predict the future, damn it. Here's how you do it . . .

> Start with a clear head and a sense that everything that's happened in the last couple of years is about to fall away, whether you want to pick at the dead skin or not. Then take an overarching peek at what's ahead—while knowing that the conventional wisdom is totally wrong.

After that, you laugh a lot at everything you've lived through—and some of us even have to take a gander at those horrible haircuts of the 1970s to remind ourselves that mistakes are meant to be remembered, chuckled at, then forgotten forever.

For the cherry, you dust yourself off and start anew, using the tools you have learned from everyone you listen to and believe in. If those people are saying anything resembling the truth, you are in good shape.

So that's what 2011 is: an exploration of trends that will affect our lives and a sense of what we have to overcome just before we leap into the new about-to-be-filled space. Or, as Woody Allen once said: "A kind of void, you know, an empty one."

And now the news: I don't want to predict a thing—not really. Regardless of what the soothsayers you read have been saying (and think about it: a book? Are you kidding? How old-world is this thing, anyway?), prediction of even the simplest events is extremely difficult and at best a finger in the air. What am I going to do, predict new types of cities and world-views and sex and networking and the dance between workers and employers, yada yada? Or, particularly, forecast how we all change constantly? Then there're the topics I have chosen: notorious people and famous places, social movements, eco-logical ideals, communication issues, artistic thoughts, sex for the ages, science, and all that outlandish tech. Predicting all that is just impossible.

What I'll do, rather, is explain and forecast a range of possi-ble futures for the subject, which is what will begin happening around the year 2011 and beyond—create a map, rather than a specific one-dimensional destination!

Most books build credibility by employing a tone of absolute authority and driving away any shadow of uncertainty. When I am working in fields where one can make credible projections or where there are accepted techniques for long-term fore-casts, I will speak with confidence and say you can't stop this.

But a kind of majestic confidence is false—fake, actually. (See the chapter in part nine called "Self Something or Other," on arti-ficial confidence.) On the contrary, it is imperative that I admit once and for all that looking into the future is an uncertain busi-ness—except for certain people who read magic eight balls with uncanny ability. Here I explain to you, already doubting reader, why this is so and why it can be a cause for anxious hope.

Ah, yes, "the futurist." How dull. I know there's this woman Faith who does it—she's good at what she portends, although a long time ago we sat together in her gorgeous duplex (triplex? I didn't get past floor one), and I got the impression that she wasn't that into her work. A little bored. I'm excited by every-thing, and that's how I'm different. Please see FrankPretzel.com for more differences—or a laugh ("Are you having a laugh?").

Besides, she runs a strategic trend-based marketing consul-tancy. How dopey is that (the dumb version of dopey)? My per-sonal goal is to rid the world of that kinda jargon.

So, am I a futurist? I guess so. Since the publication of *TrendSpotting* in 2002, I've been told I am—by the major and minor media, and by a host of influentials. But I don't believe in clichés and run from them with my legs flailing!

The book did a good job of looking ahead for you (and me). A book teaching folks how to look ahead for business calls for intelligent, grounded speculation, and of course professional expertise was the call of that day. I am not really as much futuristic as I am a show-off: I want you to use this stuff that I've gathered and realized to chart possibilities.

Here is what we will talk about in these pages.

Will this book tell you about the future? More than anything, it's loaded with topics: ideas to spur you on, move you in certain directions, and inspire you to look ahead.

• We all will work while we're sleeping. Gosh, are all these new products going to be, ahem, utilized in hours when we're supposedly adrift in our dreams? So no more wasted hours for us suckers!

• Self-involvement evolves into an art form. What used to be gross and looked down upon—self-aggrandizement— becomes in no uncertain terms beloved and coveted. Everyone wants to be like David Geffen.

• Slow attention span takes precedence. ADD peaks. We begin to take a backseat to speed, and the sudden craze is, "Why rush? We have all the time in the world." Some businesses are born; others are down!

• Customer service finally becomes law. That's enough of being put on hold. After years of thinking silently, a new movement is afoot: it's an adhered-to policy to take care of the paying folk!

• Look forward to "turn of the decade syndrome," where we reboot our lives. Come January 2011, the actual start of a new decade (and not a moment too soon, y'all) is upon us. Everyone prepares madly—just like Y2K, but positively—and uses it to make the one change to themselves that they've been desperate to achieve. So quit, start, redo—or forgive. It all happens on that very day!

• There's a movement to stay at home that occurs because—there's no real explanation, so why fake it? Our friends are more relaxed and friendly there.

You'll notice that each chapter is short, seriously so. That's what you want, and belaboring 70 or 90 topics seemed really dull and unnecessary.

I can't introduce this with any more babble. I will say, parenthetically, that this book is *all about me*, and anyone who has problems with that should skip quickly to the "Self Something or Other" chapter and see why you won't get anywhere complaining about it. So let me finish with a semisensible thought.

The future of the future is a huge idea. It scares the crap out of me. The only way to make a book out of it (except that I'm under contract) was to give as much knowledge as my brain could muster, and try to leave out nonsense that I found fascinating when I honestly knew that it was only me who got what it was—or cared.

A lot of changes happened the second I handed this manuscript in. That's why I was late, guys: just kept putting it off.

So I'm promising readers—and particularly skeptical non-believers—that I'll update as much of this as I can on Laermer.com every week. Hold me to it. After 13 books, I have a track record for remaining prolific, verbose, and no holds barred.

And I can be reached at you@Laermer.com.

On that thankfully tiny note, welcome to a business book for the day after tomorrow, a day that is fast approaching. Hope this provokes you to do something, maybe even bend the pages.

part one

TRENDSPOTTING FOR THE NOVICE

The Next Few Years Are All Wondrous

I don't want this to be like those dance cuts that make you wait forever for the beat. So with that kind of stuck in my head, here I go:

A few years ago, I was having a talk with a buddy who said she didn't care about anything new. She was content with her life. She was completely mystified by all the new stuff out there. It made her anxious. Thought, what if we could talk about the future without . . .

Boring people to death

Using jargon

Making folks go, "Who the hell cares?"

And mostly . . .

Getting them anxious!

When someone feels intimidated, it's so over. The mind turns off, and that guy is finished with you. It's like the passenger who was told, "Land the 707 and don't worry about the controls." Since so many of today's trends are related to *something* technological, it's just too much to take in. Youth-oriented ideas rule, right, so it's just hard to keep up. Nay, it's impossible to even imagine being up to speed.

> So this new book is a rambunctious and not overwhelming training manual that presents an overview of the major trends that will affect this century and explores the ways these trends will shape the global environment, technology, political life, culture, and society with a small "s."

Hey, in order to establish a framework for thinking, you've got to picture a tree (sorry, Babwa Wawa haters). The roots are technology, sure as hell, but the branches are finance, travel, weather, sex, education, communication techniques, education, gracefulness, and societal changes.

To give you a sense of the challenges we face in the coming decade, I start on a special day: January 21, 2011, 10 years after the end of the age of shamelessness. I posit that everything is new on that day.

Remember the Clinton Age? We could not stand still and yet learned very little. There was a song from my past called "We Move So Fast," from Heaven 17, that played at nineties clubs and said, to my best recollection, "We can't stand still/Alone but never lonely."

Let's take our life remote and fast-forward to where we want to learn—do better—and make some money on our knowledge. Oh, and one more prime thought: could we take a fine-tooth comb to all that conventional wisdom we've amassed ("Don't burn bridges," "Man, is Netflix a cool company!" "I really have to learn that new tech," "Gosh, it's so rude to keep canceling on her") and go forth and, as they say in the South, read

their beads. According to my friends from the Deep South, when you "read someone's beads," it means you pull down the bullshit they readily hand out, smile, and nod: "I don't think so, sugar." **It isn't necessary anymore to do what we do just because we do it.**

The purpose of 2011 is not to go out on a limb and scream or shout, but rather to manhandle the future. Predicting even relatively simple events is extremely difficult; predicting the kinds of events this book will discuss—the futures of nations, social movements, ecological systems, art and science, and so on—is impossible. I wish to explain a range of possible futures for its subject: to create a map rather than a specific destination.

Whereas most books build credibility by employing a tone of absolute authority and driving away any uncertainty, I say, what's the point? When we're working in fields where we can make credible projections, let's jump in head first. But majestic confidence sucks. On the contrary, it is imperative that I admit that looking into the future is as uncertain as all getout—and explain to readers why this is so, and why it can be a cause for hope as well as anxiety.

By making clear what we can and can't know about the future, and what forces will act to shape the future, I can offer two things of value besides a good laugh here and there. First, this book can help readers think like futurists. Second, I can help readers see what parts of the future can be shaped and changed. Perhaps the biggest difference between the ancient art of fortune-telling and modern futurism is that the fortune-tellers sought to identify events that were inevitable, while futurists—even ones who, like me, scoff at the notion—are interested in revealing the contingencies of the future: making clearer how human choice and action can make the difference between one future and another.

A book teaching folks how to look ahead for business calls for intelligent, grounded speculation, and of course professional expertise. The challenge is not to predict the future so much as to show readers how to think about and forecast and chart possibilities for the future. The book talks about the pop quizzes on our Laermer.com site. The reason is: let's see if anything sticks!

Let's keep in mind (whatever's left of it) that fundamentals shape a subject's present and can be relied upon to affect its future as well. Thoughtful experts think more credibly about the future of their subjects than they realize. That's what I'm trying to do: gather information for businesspeople on topics that will enlighten you, amuse the shit out of you, and make you go, "Wait!"

Mediocrity...

TREND: Mediocrity is ending in the next year or so, as soon we amble out of the 2000s.

Tennessee Williams taught us how most people live within the exigencies of despair. Sometime during the current decade, I realized he wasn't kidding—not a bit.

These days, everyone I know seems to be waiting for something—which is the bad news.

A lot of people don't want to admit it, but there isn't a lot that's terrific happening to us in the late 2000s, and there hasn't been for a while now. There is a lot of news about starlets in Hollywood, an anxiousness around what's happening in Washington, D.C., a lot of talk about building a skyscraper at Ground Zero, much discussion on the atrocities in Africa, and—well, nothing that grounds us or makes us go, "Wow, it's all so wonderful now." It's simply not.

I look at the situation as a sort of international inertia—the years spent waiting for a reason to unite us. Us? I mean, who doesn't want to feel connected to lots of other humans? Right now you are not, and you can't say you are—sorry, nope, don't believe you. There's hardly anything you can do about it except turn off the radio, shut off cable news, and avoid reading any media, which isn't advice I'd give anyone who wants to remain "on"!

See, there's a low buzz coming from the news media now, one that is kind of like white noise. It's there in the background; you can pick it up only when you think about it.

When you consider the buzz, you realize, uh-oh, there is no glue. Nothing connects people. We aren't learning, aren't connected, have no value system to speak of, and our kids (it always comes back to them) are desperate to be rock stars or Internet famous—not scientists, teachers, engineers, or president of the United States.

If you spend time considering what gets us *up*, it's normally something galvanizing—a bolt from the blue, I guess (see the chapter "Bolts from the Blue")—that fills us with a communal sense of worth and, if you'll forgive my one bout of New Agedness, drives us toward goals as a planet. I remember Y2K, and how frightened people were that the whole world would spin out of control. What an optimal time to be a computer nerd!

Decades past stood for something. The 1950s were black and white and family values, the 1960s rotated the world into for and against government, the 1970s were the me decade, and the 1980s introduced high finance and the first roar of technology. The last decade of the millennium past was pure mania. The economies of the world lifted us to uninterrupted heights—everything was possible.

For me, it's 1989 that stands out as seminal. I remember running to Berlin as the Wall began to get chipped away (come see the piece I have on my—yes, I have one—mantel), and at that moment we all thought there was hope for a peaceful something or other. In America, it was warmth toward European brothers and sisters, whose communal lack of apathy was mind blowing, inspiring, and something to wish for our own.

What happened? The entire decade of the 2000s until now has been—with a single clear exception, and you know which one—about nothing. The way I see it: one long *Seinfeld* episode. Rather than blather on proving this to you, since I don't have to—this is my book—I would rather introduce you to a future that, according to my projections, forecasts, and consideration via driven research and gads of experience, is going to be all about motion, action, hope, and change.

The opposite of inertia.

So get on your feet. It's time to welcome 2011, a year and a state of mind. (Well, at least I hope so.)

It was 10 years ago, on January 20, 2001, that U.S. President William J. Clinton left office. His years were unbelievable—in the truest sense. I didn't live in the 1920s, but after living as a dot-com thousandaire during that Clintonian heyday, I can only imagine . . .

Because of the nonstop economy and the bizarre technological brilliance that lay before us, golly gee, nothing was impossible. Heck, you should have been in my office during those years, when people got *funding* for ideas that were never going to make any money even if stupid people bought into them. The people who came to my firm (we do PR representation) were each more brazen than the last. No one stopped to consider that so much of the "work" they were doing was, to say the least, without boundaries or morals.

It was, to say the least, funny.

It was also a time that most of us remember as the era of shamelessness. (If you dare to admit it.) The free world's fearless leader was certainly no help. He was the man whose laissez-faire attitude about his own foibles (not meaning politics) made people think nothing was out of bounds and acceptable behavior was for others—up for grabs.

What a strange period that was, one where people told one another and our emboldened, faceless media pretty much anything they felt like saying! It was enlightened entitlement, where a 23-year-old got told that the stock he was being handed in lieu of money was "gonna be" worth millions; the stock was colorful toilet paper someone had signed, like the Deputy paper placards given to kids in police stations waiting for Mommy.

The adults in business acted the fool. Those of us who, ahem, partnered with them held fast and hoped for the best. Decisions were made on the fly. No one cared. These were sure enough the streets paved with gold our ancestors had hoped for—only most of the folks who got funded could not really explain the business they were in.

Explain away, yeah; tell the truth, hardly.

Yes, you knew it wouldn't last, and now we know. What did we learn through the years of mediocrity?

Turn the page.

In the 2000s, after burst and worst, the mediocre times set in, and books like *The Secret* took over the shelves while "comedians" like Dane Cook and Kathy Griffin creeped us out and expensive and hardly thought out TV series were created about 30-second ad characters. Worse, we allowed reality TV and unbearable movie sequels plus Simpsons-esque (Jessica, not O.J.) culture to thrive in our midst. No one knew what to do about it, and the order of the day was not to excel at much—it was about getting by and figuring out what to do next.

Most people scratched their head and said, "Give me something!" Or, as Peggy Lee whispered wistfully: *Is that all there is?*

And oh boy. All the while an endless war got started that still makes no sense to a majority. Here, I'll do it just once and lay out everything for you . . . Katrina, the horrible tsunami, MRSA infection, California fires, no toothpaste on airplanes—huh? I saw an airline pilot, infuriated, being interviewed by a major newspaper saying, "You know, I could roll this aircraft over in a minute, and nobody could stop me. But God forbid I should want to brush my teeth."—and no way out of mediocrity. The bad news got worse, international politics got stranger, our own social skills deteriorated with every IM and poorly spelled e-mail, and soon everyone was walking down the street staring at an eye-straining tiny screen.

Mediocre is stating it subtly, so let's settle on shitty as more apt.

The old wisdom said that this decade would eventually matter and somehow we'd be "trending" toward something of value. Blah . . . blah . . . blah.

Whatever passes for conventional wise-assology has been wrong about pretty much everything. How can we be moving toward something good when it's a fact that all the people we admire are obsessed with making us admire them? I know a lot of people watch Danny Bonaduce because he's a train wreck, but by giving the crazed ex-actor, ex-junkie, ex-DJ, ex-human a platform, we empower the fellow.

It makes no sense, since most people admit to being ashamed of all this banality. Ask the person sitting next to you what's the most important part of his or her life. It's not a mission to succeed at something—a rarity—and it could even be making it through the day. It's like Tennessee said, and I think maybe 1950s icon Auntie Mame stated it better: life is a banquet, darling, and most poor suckers are starving.

On the way to the banquet I predict for 2011 and beyond, this book will disprove what I call the regular irregularities that we observe. And please forgive me as I crack up at what seems to be crucial to lots of you.

Say good-bye to media as we know them, celebrities we can't stop worshipping, technology we spend our lives glancing at, and the dumbness we talk about every day. If I'm right, we might even stop chattering about the weather instead of real issues.

Good speed toward a new decade where, yep, you get to live looking forward and with healthy cynicism—and a sense of pride in what you accomplish, whom you do this with, and how you do it. Imagine, finally, connecting to people on topics you care about, rather than blabbering.

I end this discussion with a word to the freaked out: there's nothing wrong with diminishing the importance of one whole decade.

I've been on Earth for 40 years plus. I can't remember when a ten-year period got all the way to eight without getting a name. *Can you?*

We Are Not Alone

Today, for the first time I can remember, commerce is more important to us than culture—and no one expects it to be any different. Perhaps that's the sincerest definition of mediocrity.

Sam Smith, writer, activist, and social critic at the forefront of political ideas since the 1950s, is a soft-spoken, award-winning alternative journalist and editor at *Progressive Review* who sees the need for countercultures, but who sees the younger generation as not being taught how to move. "Teach people they are not alone," he offers as a solution. "That as a result of having places to meet, counterculture, artistic expression representing people outside the norm." He says, if you are part of, say, a movement, like jazz in the 1950s, you can act on it.

"Spirit of art is important when trying to find a counterculture," says Smith. He thinks the Washington rallies of the 2000s have been highly organized, "and surprising and quite impressive. But this was not like 1960s rallies. We lack the emotional side. We have no rebellion."

Sad. Yet what would it be like if we all looked up one day and said, "Time for a change"?

What would that look like? we wonder. Messy, for sure. It might make us more apt to question everything around us. Dangerous world, yeah.

Whatever happened to reading? We don't read books. We read whatever people hand us—*we are skimming from the top*. Wow, look at how much information is there for the taking. Free, yours or ours, just for being alert. Any true media junkie obsessively keeps up with the daily newspaper and weekly magazine world, particularly since so many of them are endangered species. As Jefferson remarked once in a moment of wistfulness: "Were it left to me to decide whether we should have a government without newspapers, or newspapers without a government, I should not hesitate a moment to choose the latter."

Choose to read up on the crap you've been sent—every now and then remove your eyes from your Video iPod. Read or write letters to the editor (the original user-generated content!) and raise your fists with glee. Pour through stacks of fire-hazard-making *New Yorker*s and get them inside you. Fundamental, sure, but it sure makes you a better catch at parties.

Loaded Question: Are We Futuristic, Lazy, Myopic, or Being Turned Stupid?

It's a wonderful future, and we're just starting to enjoy it now. We are, as Charlie Crews calls it, "living in the future" on NBC's unfathomably good series *Life*, sure to be canceled any second now. We all think some freaking switch will be turned and suddenly all those *Jetsons/Logan's Run/Futurama* devices will take over our lives. But the wise among us know it's all very subtle. Changes will happen, and they will be natural, just like we all took to the ways in which ones and zeroes took over our lives in the 1990s. Who would have believed that you could push a button on a browser and ice cream would appear at your door in under an hour—and cheaply too?

When I walk into a public restroom, it appears that those futuristic ideas are already here: the door opens automatically, a light shifts on, the water flows when I stick my hand in it, the mirror is in the direction of the stander (the guy next to you has his own), then I "go number one" and it flushes, the towel pops down as I go to it—gee, where's Rosie the Robot to wipe my . . .?

I walk back out—the door opens again—and then I stand on a moving sidewalk because it doesn't want me to do *anything*, and I go to a store where I'm scanning my own groceries, putting a handprint on my car to open the door, having the car talk to me, and . . . you get the message.

No? How about elevators that already know where you're headed, so they go directly there, USB ports vacuuming your keyboard, ovens that cook and turn and do it all by timer, including online calling to say, "Stick a fork in me; am I done?"

Yes, you're waiting for the car that floats, and that, my friends, is already here, but before we can get that to work, we need our politicians to change the highway system, and those gentle people, according to thinkers like Dean "Segway" Kamen, are the real holdups. So flying on the roads may take some time. But you can get anything you need delivered to you within 24 hours—and smart sites like Amazon.com have figured out how to get something to you the same day by partnering with local (read desperate) merchants who get a piece of the action just for making you, the payer, happy today.

We aren't far from George Jetson's brightly lit megawatt society. We *are* far from being satisfied by the new. In a new bathroom, try to get cold water to brush your teeth with. It's not happening.

GUMBY

THE MASCOT OF 2011

TREND: People discover that flexibility is among a few basic qualities in which to excel.

In the 1950s and 1960s, the green Gumby and his pal Pokey were TV fixtures as they joyfully lived the adventures that kids dreamed of: going to the moon, jumping in and out of books' fanciful tales, hanging with people from far-off lands. Because Gumby was a Claymation creation, he was eminently flexible and had a special knack for getting into, out of, and through fantastic and often danger-filled escapades.

> Gumby is more than ever becoming a key to success in whatever world you tool around in.

Gumby lives on in all of us—at least in those who can wipe away the thought, "I can't." Gumby's power is more than flexibility, though. The next time a colleague, a friend, or Aunt Bertha asks how you of all people triumphed in the face of some unbelievable odds, tell her, "Gumby." If she runs off looking for the latest gadget code-named for our little green hero, let her go. If she asks, "What do you mean, my young niece . . . ?"

Gumby is attitude. Snarky is so fashionable; popular culture lauds Gawker and its cadre of follower blogs and downloaders that pride themselves on carefully crafted sarcasm and forever cynicism. Gumby is confident, ambitious, and willing to get the job done—that's the essence of "Gumbitude." Gumby is optimistic and focuses on solutions—not problems. You call it like it is . . . and then you are willing to get how others see it.

Gumby is action. Lazy is easy. Action is often strenuous and sometimes exhausting, but those who have Gumby (or saw him on TV, and not the Eddie Murphy persona!) know that taking the effortless path rarely gets you where you need to be.

Identifying nascent trends, for example, requires vigorous analysis of information from multiple sources, searching beyond your comfort zone.

Gumby is results. Gumby the flexible character was all about getting the job done—both well and in a timely fashion—by effectively using all tools available. Gone are the days when tasks came with a "when you can get to it" deadline. If you're lucky enough to remember the office euphoria when IBM introduced the Correcting Selectric, then your head probably spins at the plethora of tools available to office workers in this era. These machines and doodads can help or hinder, and Gumby is all about knowing how to use them to deliver results that have a measurable impact on a noncliché bottom line, whatever your department.

Gumby learns. In each of his escapades, Gumby got an education from those around him. He sought information and explanations; he had fun figuring it out. Today, we're bombarded by data from more sources than we can count, and those who embrace Gumby invest the energy to constantly expand their wealth of knowledge.

Those who have Gumby participate. They do not sit idly by and watch from the sidelines, for they are the few who jump in and use their wit and intellect to get *any* job done, never clucking or wondering if it's in their job description or should they pass it off to someone "stupider" or "lower on the chain."

Gumby fans overcome the most troublesome glitches and find innovative solutions. Gumby isn't yes or no; it's how and why.

Ask anyone from the Air Force, who will tell you without blinking that on day two, someone told him that no matter what, "Remember that nothing is a problem."

In the military I'm told they say it with fortitude: *Semper Gumby!*

The New Way to Say Shove It!

TREND: There will be an innovative way to say, "Take this job" in the future, and I'm thrilled about its no-holds-barred emergence.

Forget your old conceptions of the workplace and imagine a place that happens to be where you work, where you can make bargains with your employer based on the fact that, yeah really, you don't *have* to work there. Because you found a place that lets you work at home—a home environment that you design with ease!

The workplace of the VNF—very near future—is going to be a big den of wonderfulness that makes your nursery school appear second grade–like.

Allow me some backtracking. In this service economy, unless they're working in a car lot, most people can work from home or anywhere. But in order for the best people to truly work at capacity in a serviceable business, they have to interact with one another.

In the coming years, workers will start to realize—thanks to the double whammy of technological advancements and knowing how good they are—that they really don't have to be at work per se to get a ton done.

You do, however, have to be responsible.

In a study that I unveiled (i.e., read about online), it turns out that we all lie about how much we work anyway: a University of Cincinnati group found that "we act all macho about our work hours," but we exaggerate more than we do anything.

Today, according to workplace types, over 40 percent of all businesses allow some sort of telecommutation. But that's usually to make life easier for working moms and people who beg for this benefit.

Along comes the—um—aging generation of workers we used to call X, boys and girls who are really knowledgeable about how to disguise where they work. Pretty soon those people are going to work at home whether or not you want them there. But as any decent employer knows, without interaction or the overused term *brainstorming*, people are not really giving their all: home work is just workplace masturbation.

So upcoming office features will be comfy dining room setups, cool makeshift kitchens—like those in the sixties-era Auto Train—and terrific designs that will make people actually want to leave their house for the sanctity of the office.

Besides nifty paints and cool-as-heck chairs, the technology in these offices will be upgraded so that phones will be easy-to-wear cordless headset devices, people will be able to move their cubicles any which way, there will be TVs to tune into, stereos and DVDs to make their day creative (or seem to do so), and there won't be a conference room per se, but a lot of areas where people can stand and say what they want to each other—quickly and without descent into non-workspeak—at giant Japanese high tables all over the fluffy space.

What does this mean for the old workforce throughout the world? As the economy improves from a period of "quixoticity," this will not be a 1990s-style tug of war where people left good jobs for better ones. It'll be, "You want me? Make my digs tons of fun, or I am working at home . . . like all my slobbish friends do."

> Go to work wherever you are, get it done, prove your value, and then go dancing. Do the frug! (www.webref.org/dance/f/frug.htm) (found on Laermer.com/dances)

No One Reads the Manual and Why

Soon after my mini-opus *trendSpotting* was released in 2002, I did a series of TV programs on why no one reads the (fucking) manual that comes with a new product. Here are the reasons derived—explaining why thinking is so gauche and outré now.

1. People don't like to read.

2. People think they know everything anyway—having to RTFM may mean that they are not really the experts they think they are.

3. Manuals are too hard to read—or have too many pages—or don't have enough sexy pics inside.

4. The product described in the manual is poorly designed, so it *needs* an instruction manual, which makes us think horribly of it and gives us buyer's remorse.

5. People are lazy.

6. **People are dumb.** This you need me for?

7. People are impatient.

8. People can't find what they need quickly enough.

You know, what's funny is that in the end, it all comes back to technology. If you make something really easy and table-dumbed-down (see "Terms I Made Up + Newfangled Future Speak"), you won't have a problem getting us all to learn what you proffer. We'll share our newfound easy knowledge with everyone, who will share it with their "everyone"!

I think easiness will become a thing of the future. In the United States, Ikea, which produces hard-to-pronounce furniture that is cheap and a little reliable, has always had a problem: it's impossible to put the pieces together. Recently, Ikea took a step in the right direction. Rather than reprint a thousand Swedish-style manuals for the manual-averse, the company simply hired handymen in many corners of the United States and offered to have them come to your place, at a reduced rate, to make sure your furniture isn't missing any sides.

Anyway, I asked one hell of a groovy friend of mine what he thought about the above. "I go out a lot," he explained, "and I always need help getting there. So we were in the car last night when I was out to dinner with friends, and as we finished dinner and were waiting for the car to be brought from the garage, I pulled my cell out of my pocket, dialed *JAM for a traffic report, told the guy where we were, and asked for the best route out of the city; in 30 seconds a guy told me the Yankees game was about to let out, the Holland Tunnel had a tube blocked, and the 36th Street entrance to the Lincoln Tunnel had a five-minute wait.

"The woman we were with was blown away, and then I knew that boy technology changed everything. What were you saying?"

part two

THE CABOODLE: ADVANCED TRENDSPOTTING

DIVE INTO TRENDS . . . AND BELIEVE IN THEM

TREND: Everything is useful when you wish it to be.

Fool me once, shame on you. Fool me twice, shame on me. Fool me three times—you have a trend that's about to take off.

A trend is something that is just beginning to happen—the way ads are becoming smaller by the second; the use of tiny devices that are almost ear-sized for us to check who wants to reach us; the tendency for movies to be built around consumer products like Ben Stiller's haircut or a particular type of Mercedes (crap slogans, wicked cars)—and that is happening in a significant enough way to portend real and widespread change.

The trends that are ostensibly enjoyed by a few lucky people now will be experienced by a good many tomorrow and virtually everyone next week. And a good trendspotter knows how to separate the wheat from the chaff, how to distinguish today's passing fancy or fading passion from tomorrow's hot new item du jour.

In lots of businesses—media, entertainment, PR and marketing, fashion, and all financial type professions—knowing the latest trend is a prerequisite for success or survival. The message is clear: you miss out on a trend, and you're out on the street.

> Or, as I tend to put it, do it now and stay alert or have the person who replaces you do it for ya!

Trendspotting is a viable way of spending your time even if you're not in these industries: "Are you ready for the road of life?" asked an old Mazda ad. Car commercials used to sell you sex appeal and power—now they promise that you will be equipped for "the road of life," one that apparently leads to an unknown and terrifying future. (Although car makers themselves are all nervously "looking ahead," some variant on the words *go, forward, ahead,* and *forth* is in every car ad I see these days. Originality is in short supply.) Consumers are subject to the fear that they won't know enough to get on with their lives; they don't feel equipped to spot trends in their own lives.

I asked I ask a lot of people for advice. a journalist-slash-novelist why she thought we are so fascinated by trends. "It's simple," she said. "The trends happen, and we find ourselves in the middle of them, and we want to identify what is happening."

People need a way to identify and understand trends in order to make sense of what is happening in their lives. And what's most urgent is not to just say it's something that someone else will do.

In the middle of the last century, Presbyterian minister William J. H. Boetchker (1873–1962) lectured around the United States about the hard work and character that leads to success. I worship this guy because his work led to what he called the Seven National Crimes:

1. I don't think.

2. I don't know.

3. I don't care.

4. I am too busy.

5. I leave well enough alone.

6. I have no time to read and find out.

7. **I am not interested.** WJHB also said that the "individual activity of one man with backbone will do more than a thousand men with a mere wishbone." I sure do love him.

That's pure ignorance, and it's not an acceptable way to live. So, then, how do you move forward, and what are the tactics a businessperson must embrace in order to be the ultimate personal spotter?

1. *Market research.* Analyze your (and your competitors') place in the market and I.D. clear paths to achieving business objectives. A term that a lot of folks use now is "ethnographic trend studies," and it simply involves speaking to potential customers, current ones, media if you know any (just call), and your own sales force to get a diagnostic report on where you're at.

2. *Monitor the media, but really do it.* Comb the thing! Get clues from the social fabric below the stories and think about what the reporter or blogger is really saying. Are the people on TV just anchoring and don't have a true opinion—or are they also giving you a clue that what they are talking about is pure bullshit? Keep a close-edged monitor on what the opinion pieces say versus the news, and recognize the difference, since the former is much more important to your business. Find the subtle suggestion of a trend before it's full-blown. Then monitor the blogs that are all abuzz in your industry

and see what issues are being raised the most. How do you fit into those, or, better yet, how *could* you be in those firmly?

3. *Influencer check-ups are next.* Talk to people who fit the demographic you wish to reach, and ask them what they think of what you're doing. Then see how you can be trendier.

4. *Audits are a must!* In other words, take the influencer network you've just collected and ask the people in it lots of questions (give them something for their time, please) to zoom in on what they as a whole will most want to see from you, and ostensibly purchase from you—dig?

5. *As I mention a few times: ask the right questions.* Once you identify the influencers or fine people who really will help you get to the next step, ask them to sit still for a half hour, max, while you outline your immediate, mid-range, and long-term plans to market. Then see if there's something they respond to that's actionable—in any way useful.

6. *Share the sights.* Write a trend-oriented newsletter for your best customers and ask those customers if you are onto something with these trends or just blowing smoke. Repackage this sent-out knowledge for internal audiences, to keep them in the know (i.e., pleased with themselves).

7. *Influence the trends.* Creating and affecting trends is not an overnight thing. The key is understanding clearly what trends are out there, their roots, and how in fact they affect the target audiences' acquisition (read: buying) habits. So what can you do to shape and anticipate trends in a concrete way? Well, you can make sure that everyone in your organization is participating. Ask them to keep a diary— not one about whom they're dating but one that talks about the activities they see that are purely new. Then use free or cheap online chat rooms and do a weekly meeting where everyone shares one aspect of "the new" that they think someone outside the company would like to know about. Then go out and tell folks.

8. *Messaging, as anyone who communicates for a living will attest with vehemence, is urgent and, way too often, left to chance.* Coalesce the information and insights you have gathered and examine them in the context of your external messaging and positioning. See what's missing its bull's-eye mark.

9. *The most important rule in spotting trends is the rule of talking to experts.* Here's how:

   • Pay attention to what's around you—and particularly people you trust.

   • Ask the right questions.

   • Have faith in your sources and write down what they say. Seriously, a few notes on a piece of paper go a long way; gosh, go buy a notebook this very minute.

   • Find visionaries who can teach you new ideas, and try to tell them one thing they weren't aware of. People who are true visionaries know that they can take a new person's idea to another level. So they are thankful to respond to your call/e-mail. It's important to learn to recognize the difference between true visionaries and slick BS.

New list:

1. Pay attention to the signs that something—big change—is on the horizon. Not just the "financial porn" that is on the covers of money magazines saying "Doom" or "Yay." Really take a look around you. Are we on our way to a boom, a bust, or just another pretty mediocre period for financials? How should you prepare?

2. Great Trendspotters are always evolving, learning, and growing. Remember that Italian class you're always thinking of taking? Right.

3. Don't just read the arts or pop culture news. Be well rounded. In your own business, and in life, nothing succeeds (even success) like being knowledgeable, the one who says something that is not what is expected. Everyone remembers the smart ass.

Since You Weren't Reading Carefully, I Made Another List

Here is a sum of what you can do starting today. It has more group action—in case you didn't feel like reading before.

1. Follow leaders—pay attention.

2. Use the Net for everything (forget privacy concerns—they're nonexistent and almost funny now, so go, click, and be merry), because at any given time you can follow the thoughts of approximately 1.5 million random, just-as-fascinated people. A nice number—and one I didn't have to make up.

3. Collect data on areas that interest you. Hey, one thing that everyone forgets—and I know I said it before, but I can't stress it enough—get a napkin and write it down. Even if you don't ever look at the page again, the brain works in oh-so-mysterious ways. I do this with my always-neglected shopping lists that I don't bother with before I dial up the Chinese Delivery Guy.

4. Get on mailing lists about things that interest you. It's so easy to do that now. Gosh, in the old days you had to send SASEs (for the kids, that's self-addressed envelopes with stamps—or snail). Today you just shoot an e-mail to someone or click a link. I mean, jeez, there's no excuse.

5. Use separate e-mail addresses just to collect separate information. Get a Hotmail or Gmail account for spam. In these cases, e-mail is—dare I say it—worthy.

6. Subscribe to trade publications. Man, you can get so many of them gratis. In trade magazines you read passionate and often interesting articles on things you had heretofore thought were dull. Plus, you get to see others work hard to explain what you found inexplicable.

7. Talk to experts—arrange to meet. I've said it before, and I will say it again.

8. Don't ignore indicators. In 1929, the only ones who made it through the crash were those who read newspapers. And really read 'em. By the way, myyahoo.com and mywashingtonpost.com—all that stuff you think you want to know—are not good enough. Expand your wings, broaden personal focus, all those other clichés . . .

9. Just do it over and over again. Nike had a point, albeit a repetitive one.

10. It is indubitably a must to be informed. But come on, talking about being interested in order to succeed is so obvious. If you don't know this, then close the book. Today, it's more urgent than ever to be interest*ing* since that would put you in a class by yourself—people tend to like you better because you are a hotbed of "hmm, cool fact" in a society where people repeat the same one-liners daily. *It is better to be remembered for who you are than simply nodded at.*

11. Stay awake. I like my lattes with lowfat.

FAD, FADDY, AND FATTENING TRENDS

TREND: Fads are take-it-or-leave-it. Don't for a second ignore trends that portend a lot.

Every day someone asks me, what's the diff? You've got fads and trends, and they all seem to amount to the same thing. Fads are everyday occurrences that you go "ah" at and then forget about. So, my fine friends, no. A fad is a flash in the pan that doesn't even deserve mention in a book like this; a trend is something that foretells widespread change for us in a culture that can't stand still.

A trend is something that is just beginning to percolate—but is happening in a significant enough manner that we can see how it's going to change us. Somehow.

To enforce a point, trends enjoyed by a few today will be experienced by many tomorrow and by all in a bit. Gosh, I really hope someone is listening.

A trend is what is about to hit. I can't keep stressing how much you have to be alert to notice something that will, wow, get everyone moving in the same direction. That is what to look for. When you've got a single example, it's a noticeable situation. When you have two of the same, that's a fact, sir. And when you have three examples, call it a trend. I'm sure I said this earlier, but whatever. That's something you need to remember.

A good trendspotter knows how to separate the wheat from the chaff, how to distinguish today's passing fancy or fading passion from tomorrow's something hot.

As I wrote the last chapters of this book, I sniffed out a trend: live television. You laugh and think, "Richard, what are you talking about? That's been here since the 1950s." Not really—mostly it's been in spurts. But recently, Bill Maher's live show and the as-it-happens *Dancing with the Stars* both received tons of ratings and attention because of accidental and exciting moments that could not be choreographed or rehearsed, namely people shouting terrible non sequiturs (the worst kind of non) at Maher in his HBO studio and Miss Marie Osmond fainting after a particularly showy number. We Trendspotters can tell that in the coming years, those two events—which happened within days of each other—have set in motion the live television that will get executives in TV World's blood boiling. Ratings? On television? It's almost quaint. But good business is always good business.

I can't stress enough that trends are boiling under the surface every day and we find ourselves in the midst of them, and yet only some of us can identify what happened! People need to I.D. and understand trends because we want to make sense of what's happening in our already complicated lives. That is what I call trendy. Everything else is talk, talk, talk—and promotional nonsense.

If you're good at this, you can spot the faux trends, when someone makes it seem like the percolation has begun and all he truly wants is for you to buy something.

Bandwagoning

You know how we're always being told to *do things better*, to *try harder*, to *reinvent*, to *reengineer*, to *break the rules*, to *innovate*, to *make a difference*? You know how "good" is never good enough? How we're made to feel guilty for doing what's been done before, for taking the well-trodden path? Just look at some wow-selling book titles: *Good to Great*; *First, Break All the Rules: What the World's Greatest Managers Do Differently*; *The Goal: A Process of Ongoing Improvement*.

Well, maybe there's just a chance that it's OK to follow in others' footsteps. Not to reinvent the wheel, but instead to roll with it. Maybe we can live better, saner, even more successful lives by jumping on the bandwagon, not sitting at the reins trying to blaze the trail ourselves. I call it *bandwagoning*. It's succeeding in your goals in a way that feels more natural . . . some might even say in a "lazy" way.

Here is my definition of *bandwagoning*: it's the lazy person's way to success. But don't let the "lazy" part put you off. I don't mean lazy in a bad way, or, rather, I don't necessarily think that being lazy is bad. In fact, I think that being lazy can be positively good for you. There is pseudoscientific evidence that being lazy not only is beneficial to the spirit and to our general well-being, but can actually make us more successful. Successful according to all the usual criteria such as wealth and happiness!

So please justify all things that are the path of least resistance in life, whether at home or at work, that feel right for good reason. Demonstrate to everyone that taking naps, bucko, is good, nay, a brilliant part of everyday life and leads to greater productivity. Watching TV opens your eyes to the world and provides undreamed-of moneymaking opportunities—those Ginzu knives must be making someone real cash! We'll give you tips on how to avoid unwelcome social contact and how to survive when you're traveling away from home. Recognize that, as a bandwagoner, you'll be ahead of the curve, and not everyone will be accepting of your new stress-free way of life; you can now proudly cover up so as to appear suitably frenetic and driven.

BOLTS FROM THE BLUE

TREND: More than ever, we will wait for something to send us home from our tedium.

Conventional wisdom suggests that people from my home country—America!—outwork everyone else. We are entirely consumed by our jobs—a nation of PDA-addled workaholics with no "off" button that we admit to. Which proves that Marshall McLuhan was wrong when he said decades ago that in 20 years the only words Americans would know would be *on* and *off*. We work on the weekends. We take no vacations. We compete to wake up first, go home last, and take the briefest breaks. Our jobs make us Job. It's as though offices have replaced Employee of the Month with Martyr of the Month. Today's new recruits may as well include on their résumés a line underscoring their proficiency in Word, Excel, and masochism. It's become factory standard.

Until there is a Bolt from the Blue. Allow me a little literary license. I'm not talking about *real* lightning striking you.

On September 11, 2001, this nation stopped. Even Starbucks closed its shaken, not stirred, Manhattan doors! What *could* people do, or companies do, except huddle around the nearest set for warmth? The events were too overwhelming, the stakes too high, work too freaking unimportant. Eventually we drifted back to the office—eventually—and things returned to what might be called normal. Unless that office was in Washington, D.C. Everyone there went through the looking glass.

While such a reaction to the specific 9/11 events was appropriate, it demonstrated a larger sociological pattern that seems to have surfaced in office culture in the States.

When something—anything—happens "out there" in the world at large, your world (the usual flow of TPS reports and PowerPoints) halts with a screech. We—the great workforce, the most suffering in the history of office dronedom—simply stop. And this needs to be analyzed.

By me.

The tragedies of 2001 themselves explain a part of this phenomenon. To a certain degree, we now exist in a kind of permanent shell shock, which I have to admit was good for a while because it shocked us into thinking smarter, but for how long do we need it? The 9/11 was our Bolt to end all bolts, a disaster whose scale and immediacy robbed us of such luxuries as indifference or detachment, at least for a while.

It happened, it can happen again, and it is bound to happen again. If we don't think that way, then something else will. In the years to follow, things that felt big—a sudden citywide blackout or devastating downpour or manhole explosion—could no longer exist in any humanmade vacuum.

Now, there's a chance that "it" could be another It, another Day X from which point everything changes. So whereas there was a time before 2001 when the afore-talked-about *underreacted* to the world's very real dangers, we now overreact to any and all possible moments that could make us go home.

Everything's a touch more fragile, and our psyches are a little frail.

> And so we anticipate disaster, and when it doesn't quite strike, we feel as though we should at least go home and ponder what might have been.

Gosh, imagine, if in fact that JetBlue plane had crashed on the day everyone ran to the TV to watch it land. And when it didn't, I'm fairly sure those who went to their domiciles to watch it . . . were disappointed.

Bolts also play into a culture that's oversaturated with media and still unsure of how best to use them. When Capital-B Bolts struck in the last decade of the millennium (bombs hitting Baghdad, bullets hitting Columbine, Waco, and a lot that lay on the side of those devastating moments), we gathered around a still-fresh-gifted glow of cable news, and we now had hours and hours to process the disaster of the day from every angle (it's on the menu).

There were moments—like when a certain former football star heard the first verdict—when everything ground to a halt. (I stayed away from that, though I admit to staying home to hear Michael Jackson's verdict, mostly because of the head-shaking quality of the trial.) However, in the 1990s, there was some balance to our Bolt reactions.

Our trained media fed us everything we wanted but mostly let us have days off.

Around the time of the earlier paragraph's parenthetic trial mention, we became oversaturated and captivated devourers of the 24-hours-a-day content-creator nation. Everyone has a camera or a blog, and everyone is a bringer of information or opinion. Let's just be honest: who the fuck can tell the difference? Everyone has an outlet—and it's one that we are paying attention to, or someone is. We have an awful lot of digital space to fill.

Every event must be magnified to do its job. We hop from not-so-jarring fluff to not-so-jarring fluff, mining Google News for the next cycle, believing history to be forged by giant events and shocking moments that give us a constant stream of themes to provide the narrative that we desperately need to get us through these dull, dull times.

Summing up, it's difficult to imagine previous generations reacting to news on the wire of Anna Nicole Smith's demise like it was the *Titanic* or the *Hindenburg* (unless it was a national tsking at morals run amok). (Similarities among the three events are entirely incidental.) And so, whereas true Bolts used to be genuinely shocking and therefore the only news worth reporting—think Walter Cronkite's tearful announcement of JFK's death—our news in these days of mediocre reporting and reportage has become corporatized, repetitive to within an inch of its life, homogenized, and stripped of perspective in search of a rating point. Don't you sometimes look to see what corporate entity owns the station you're listening to? And what it gets out of talking about a certain "other company" that it might own or have dealings with?

Regardless of who reports it, we take *any* cue to mean that we should stop what we're doing and pay attention.

Or, perhaps, we respond to bolts both big and small because conventional wisdom is trying to keep us sane (wise?). Maybe it is *because* we work too many hours and for too many weeks of the year that it's good for us to have a reason/excuse/ moment to stop. We live in an amped-up, nervous culture that bombards our senses and shortens our attention spans to where it's impossible to sit still without having something to do. We're all slaving away at an ambiguous information age of busywork, and when people buckle, it ought to be for a reason that at least will give us pause.

I know, and you know, that we waste astounding chunks of time compulsively checking e-mail, shopping for shoes, or playing fantasy sports. Some productivity experts tell me this is hundreds of times more costly to the U.S. economy than the Iraq War. And so what I call breaks from the drudgery tend in a way to waken us from tedious, low-energy routines.

Bolts from the blue give us a rare opportunity to connect communally for an hour or an afternoon or a week. As the dreadful decade following 9/11 has progressed, we hear a lot about how politically and spiritually unified the country was in the attack's immediate aftermath. I remember that being true. But maybe it was less about shedding our partisan stripes than it was about feeling that we'd been jarred loose from worrying about the bad economy and given a chance to look with fresh eyes at who we'd become.

I end on that note. Yes, there will be a quiz. See Laermer.com/boltfromblue. In that I will ask questions about what affected you, and you will answer them, and the winners will receive prizes. They won't be big.

The Decade Is Starting Anew— and Maybe the World Is Too

Paraphrasing Sondheim, What Else

TREND: It's the New Decade, and it's a moment made especially for you—take advantage and enjoy every bit of it!

Maybe it's because our current decade dawned with our dot-com bubble busted, that disputed election, and an unfathomable attack on American soil. Or maybe it's because so much of our attention in the following years was devoted to news too dire to digest (Iraq's consequences) and fluff too digestible to be relevant (Britney's crotch). Maybe the extraordinary successes of the 1990s (which saw, as if by magic, the Cold War fizzle and wallets fatten) left us with a hangover.

Or maybe it's because these 10 years have been so difficult to define; even before the 1960s, 1970s, 1980s, and even the hardly explicable 1990s ended, we knew what they meant.

But whatever the reason, the unnamed, awkward decade ending in 2010 seems to have served mostly as a default hiatus from our, ahem, real lives. That isn't to suggest that it's been stagnant. After all, a war is raging and the financial markets have jerked us up and down. There's renewed fervor attached to national politics. Technological breakthroughs have ushered in new models for the creation and distribution of media that have changed our information society on a Gutenberg scale.

And yet very little seems to have *really* happened. There is, more than anything else, *anticipation* of what's next, in a culture that's accelerating ever faster with each passing month. But anticipation means waiting. That is, until the calendar flips to 2011. Just as health clubs swell and cigarette sales plummet briefly every January, every decade begins with the promise of change. The decade is starting anew, so maybe you will too.

It wasn't supposed to be this way. Very rarely are grand plans announced and then achieved tidily and within the arbitrary bookends of a decade, like the space race of the 1960s. But it does seem as though, rather than answering the proverbial call, we've collectively hit the hold button.

In a certain way, the unusual nature of the last two decades might help to explain why the momentous shift into the twenty-teens is sneaking below the radar. The beginning of the decade, circa 1991, was a watershed period, as Communism had its Garbo moment and speculation was rampant concerning the end of one century and our bridge to the next. Then Y2K hype dominated the turn of the next decade. But what really sets apart the 2011 leap?

Perhaps we have created our own mass inhalation. Distraction fuels procrastination, and every trend suggests that the world is finding more and more ways to shorten its attention span and overload any leftover senses.

How easy it becomes, then, to look up every now and then from our PDAs to say that we'll be sure to get to "it"—whether "it" means committing to alternative energy policies or getting smarter or doing that Living Will or rethinking the estate tax or hitting the treadmill even once—when 2011 rolls around.

People have been waiting to start anew. I have. To take up the challenges—big and small—that have been put off for too long. It's as though we've wandered through a haze and begun to see it lift with the coming election cycle, but won't really be able to get on with our progress until we have the "excuse" of 2011. So there.

Golly, Beav, Is There a Right Way?

R un, run, run. That's all we do. In some sappy, overdramatic song from the very late 1980s, Linda Ronstadt warbled, "You just carry on and keep moving fast." This was just before the speed of the digital age took over. What did Linda see or feel? Probably that being slow (or low down) was easy if you gave a second over to what's wrong.

> People are apt to do what they do mostly because they're sure it will get them something.

That definitely wasn't the way it was in the 1970s.

Why do I choose that decade? Because there was nothing to do but think back then. And when you ponder the probabilities—as opposed to just acting on one—you are likely to do what's right. The one "thing" that in your heart you know is the route to, well, run roughshod over!

People in this strange decade have spent many years *doing* before thinking. And that has not helped us evolve. To just blurt out what's on your mind may sound like a hip thing to do, but it causes trouble. Honesty is one thing—"I want you to know"—but if you don't know that what you're saying is true, then why waste the energy?

There is a right way. A clear vision. I'm not saying that any of us have it, but you know it's out there somewhere. Being confused or beguiled or asking too many questions: that's the way it is when you squint and wonder if any of this has any meaning. I used to tell people all the time, "I'm easily confused" just to disarm them when I peppered them with queries. But I realize now that it was mostly because I didn't *buy* what people were telling me. They were in fact talking, as opposed to communicating, with me.

Clever Fran Lebowitz used to opine: "The opposite of talking is waiting." That's not funny anymore.

A slow attention span is the way of the future. The moment you sit there, turn off the computer and device, and give some thought to how you would like the world to be.

Experts I sidled up to say we will want to slow down in the near future—and the reason is: we're plumb exhausted. You can run only for so long.

STAY INFORMED BY DEPERSONALIZING

TREND: Stay informed by depersonalizing. Or, stop caring about the same things.

The goal: to find valid information underneath a decibel level that's run amok. The way: say hi to your new part-time job with bennies.

For starters, much of what we do wrong when we search for information is—search. It's not a game, and your first boo-boo is thinking that grabbing at the topic at hand is the way to dive in. Uh-uh. Don't grab; let it all come to you. But don't make the mistake of seeking out only the facts you think you're bound to need. Be broad-minded, and most of all, imagine that you know nothing when you look. Because in the end, what will give you your trend and help you forecast like the best of them is that nugget that says, "Oh my. I didn't the hell know that!"

In the 1990s, in the Gold Rush, a whole bunch of news and culture sites decided to proffer a dangerous precedent. They said to us Web wishers: don't spend all your time on our destination of knowledge and insight, pshaw. We'll *push* it to you. Suddenly the "my" life began—mynewyorktimes, myyahoo, myplayboymag, myrichardlaermer. It was a nutty time when people's e-mail boxes got inundated by the daily outflux of gobbledygook we thought we wanted. It amounted to people reading about sports and the arts. Not much else was pushed to these undiscerning masses! It's back, with municipalities throughout the world naming their sites things like mydelraybeach, mymaldives, or mypalmsprings—cute is better than obvious, I guess.

It was not a banner time for trendspotters, and it was a super dour moment for those of us who like to think we're well informed since, ack!, hardly anyone else is. So, like, who do we talk to at cocktail parties? What good is it if all your "spoutables" are areas you already know so much about? If you can't talk about new fields—if you cannot stretch into fields that are outrageously exciting and recently discovered—you're boring. Connect the dots, my friends, and before you know it you'll see that everything does come together in a world that isn't just about one thing. As a matter of fact, if you study what sports and politics have in common, you'll see it's more than cadences. Stock and art markets, not coincidentally, rise and fall at the same rate. International strife and corporate lying are strangely chartable. High finance and lowbrow culture sleep together regularly.

A hint for the curious: the trade magazines we spoke about in an earlier chapter are not just for people who toil in those fields. A trade publication is a wonderful, free, and bizarrely informational medium to learn from. Just call or write the magazine and say you want to learn. People who cover paper or call centers or direct marketing or wallpaper or libraries or garbage picking up are either *totally into* the fields they call home or desperately seeking new angles, which in fact make their magazines often incurably readable. They'll send you an issue to get you on your way—ask for a user name for the site, too (lie and say you might advertise, or don't and say you are new to the field—just flirt, be charming, insist). Then the rest is archived online, so get in! And yeah, you should have a second e-mail address so as not to clog the personal arteries. Grab all you can on whatever topic *du Web* and in no time you'll be faking it like the fine day-jobbers who work in that once unknown industry.

Last topic of this seriously helpful (and maybe a little dense) chapter: local news. It's just incredible how much you can learn from the local "throwaway rags" that I personally can't wait to get. These are chock-full of ditties that you just won't find anywhere else—at least, not until the big papers get hold of them. In 2004, the *Washington Post* reported how the *Villager*, the informative veteran free weekly in the City of New York, somehow fed dozens of stories to the *New York Times* "coincidentally" (my quotes). In other words, the article subjects appeared in the little guy and were subsequently crucially noted in New York's "newspaper of record."

What that says, and it's hardly coincidental, is that a lot that starts small ends big.

The ink-stained wretches of your community's information-gathering device know what's happening and work hard to inform you, who buy from their advertisers. They hope.

part three

The Business of Selling, as Opposed to Shilling

TREAT ME RIGHT OR YOU WON'T GET MY MONEY

TREND: Here's a risky idea. In the very near future, don't do what others do for their customers to make them feel good and a little loyal. . . . Just follow your own selfish instincts.

This is a story about Starbucks, the one revered mega-conglomerate that can do no wrong. (Not.)

I used to think, "What a relaxing, aurally regulated place to hang my hat for a few minutes in quiet comfort while I rip off a leftover paper and think about something I should." Not anymore. Now I get what Starbucks is: a crowded coffee shop that is, yes, too expensive even for someone like me who enjoys wasting money. It has become a conglomerate with a sense that it can sell anything, and we will buy it. Strangely, the CDs and movies it promotes haven't made a lot of real money.

A few summers ago, the Naked Woman Logo got burnt when it sent a "Free Iced Coffee" e-mail promotion to the myriad friends-of-Starbucks (mostly associates, executives, and colleagues) after it had a run of IC in the summer! Just after everyone started forwarding the darn things to everyone they knew, Starbucks called off the promotion. On the counters, the company placed a black-and-white sign that stated, "This was meant only for Friends and Family," to explain why it wasn't honoring the coupon any longer! Most people who saw the sign went, "Wait a minute. Well, who the fuck am I? Enemy of the state?"

I began to think, "Wait a minute. Why doesn't Starbucks offer a card program like every other bean counter I visit?" When I'm in a local coffee joint, someone throws a card at me—buy something a lot, get a serious freebie. It seems like that's something everyone is doing now. And it keeps me loyal.

I called 1-800-Starbuc and spoke with Jonah. He told me that he didn't know why the company didn't offer a buy-X-get-Y-free promotion. He presumed with honesty, "The powers that be must not have found it profitable enough." He then offered to transfer me to the media relations desk. The people there only work with v-mail; there's no live person—but they "check their messages every hour." I opted to shoot them an e-mail instead. Two days later, something else came at me from that quick "Hey, how's it going?" e-mail lobbed over the transom.

I have to say before you read it: I did not mention Safeway in my e-mail; I've never *been* in one. I'm wondering if it's a "She doth protest too much" scenario, and they're still worried about such scenarios biting them in the ass.

From: [mailto:info@starbucks.com]

Sent: Monday, August 20, 2007 1:48 PM

To: Richard Laermer

Subject: Response from Starbucks Coffee Company—Case # 4486609

Hello,

Thank you for taking the time to contact Starbucks with your comments about Safeway's "Buy 7, Get 8th On Us" promotion. We welcome questions and feedback at any time.

We apologize for any confusion regarding this promotion. It was initially set up as a limited time offer to help introduce the convenience of having Starbucks in your local Safeway. In the future Safeway will offer occasional Starbucks promotions, and I hope that you will continue to enjoy the convenience of visiting the Starbucks while shopping in your local store.

Thanks again for your interest in Starbucks Coffee. If you have any further questions or concerns, please feel free to call Safeway at 877-723-3929 to speak with a representative or to go to the Contact Us form at www.safeway.com to submit additional feedback.

Warm Regards,

Jonathan M.

Customer Relations

Starbucks Coffee Company

I had to look into that one. It turns out that there was another promotion the summer after the first debacle, a limited-time offer—one that caused much confusion on the part of the consumers who frequented the Starbucks "embedded" in Safeway. There was so much noise made as a result that Starbucks had to issue an apology letter.

These people give nothing away, it appears.

Then Bridget called me back, two days after my request to Media Relations about my buy-X-get-Y-free query.

She was not very forthcoming. Here is her reply almost word for word, condescension still in.

If you're familiar with the brand, then you'll know what the experience is like. And we're always trying to find new ways to surprise and delight our customers. Our goal is to bring that experience to customers all over the world.

Up to this point, we haven't been interested in doing [the discount card]. We haven't decided that is the best way to maintain the experience.

After providing me with this nonanswer, Bridget said if I needed more information, she would be happy to assist. But in order for her (the hip coffee place?) to help, I'd have to put in writing exactly what I would be doing with it. As if writing about the company in our sweet book isn't enough. Harrumph.

Care to follow up? I have her direct line. E-mail me. I write back in one day, and I will be sure it's your question I'm answering.

The Biggest Picture

The Customer Is a Hyperaware King

TREND: Since we are the most networked people in the history of history, you can't get away with stating anything sloppily anymore. When communicating with your customer, be careful.

The salon in Soho where I get my hair cut has been doing a terrific job for years. But it has branched out to the point of no return, and now the owner's got a whole line of products he's hawking. Whatever. But now when I call, instead of "push 1 for reservations," it's "push 1 for products." That pisses me off, and I'm considering finding a new place for a hairdo.

It makes me think about how businesses these days forget how fickle the purchaser is, and how every little public decision counts. A lot.

Let's look at Folgers, the coffee company that sells caffeine powder and has over $450 million of the market. It went out and said that a new, softer coffee would be better for the stomach—and it had the science to prove it.

Folgers called the new coffee Simply Smooth. "Made from specially selected beans that are roasted to reduce certain irritants that may affect a sensitive stomach," went the super big release.

People started going to their favorite blogs and explaining in droves that this seemed suspiciously like marketing-speak and not something that made a whole lot of sense. We call that bullshit. Then suddenly the *New York Times* (and the *Times*-owned *International Herald Tribune*) ran a quote by Dr. Joel E. Richter about it—after seeing the online ruckus. "It's as much mythology as anything," Richter blabbed. "The evidence that coffee is injurious to the stomach isn't there." That appeared on page one. . . .

How many people are now walking past Folgers for Maxwell House, where being good to the last drop was never in question. Folgers has fibbed—and P&G just said they're putting the brand up for sale!

What about the iTunes iPod iPhone Apple religion? Even Apple makes mistakes that it doesn't see how *easily* we unmask. This corporation just did something awesome that at first made me look up and say, "Wow, a business is listening." In early 2007, Apple announced that we could buy entire albums of songs we had purchased—cheaper than if we'd gotten the missing songs as singles. Brilliant. However, in micro-words, Apple explained that this was only for a limited time. But I don't understand why. What's the rush? If I own the first songs, give me as long as I want to Complete My Album, as the come-on went.

Why does a wickedly cool company like Jobs's have to be as officious as anyone else? You already have my business! (See the chapter "New Rule.")

Being careful is important; this slapdash get-it-for-you-now world is looking for buttoned-up companies that give us what we want. Strings be damned.

> I'd like to offer a suggestion: pushing the send key without thinking things through will become your biggest problem.

Since 100 percent of the population is using digital communication, they tsk-tsk bad spelling along with your perceived rudeness.

Why do people say things when they are smart enough to know that *someone* must know that this will probably get them in trouble? That is an age-old question that geniuses like us will have to answer. In *Jeopardy* fashion, the answer seems to be: "What is making people think poorly of you?"

Can an Athlete Really Be Trusted to Make Money for Us?

TREND: We need heroes to make us feel good or better; sports stars are going to be deleted as moneymakers for big companies. Leave them at play.

Celebrity athletes had better watch out. Marketers who have used these celebrities as sponsors are trying to figure out what to do.

In the year before this book was born, heroes that we had raised up found themselves in an unsettling number of unflattering situations. The Atlanta Falcons' Vick went to the dogs. San Francisco Giants' Bonds set the all-time home run record just before he was hit over the head with steroid and lying-about-it charges. Tour de France competitors were accused of doping—and one was found guilty and then loudly stripped of his title.

But Vick's story is crucial to my point. Before he went to the dogs, he was a character on- and offstage and had made deals with three major brands that were estimated to be worth $7 million annually. Nike's was the biggest. Vick also had a deal with Upper Deck, which pulled his memorabilia and cards from its site.

Nike was *not about* to do him.

Vick, like O.J. before him, may never be seen as more than an abuser. It reminds me of Mike Tyson, who did all those Diet Pepsi ads with his ex-wife, Robin Givens, before going to prison for rape and then chewing on Holyfield's ear.

Yet there's a lot of money at stake here. Sick money. According to *Promo* magazine, which interviewed me about this in 2007, the overall sports sponsorship market was projected to hit *at least* $9.9 billion that year (which is why they called), a fairly not unimpressive 10.8 percent jump over 2006.

After MasterCard stopped even thinking about sponsoring Bonds in 2006 (the ink hadn't dried on the agreement), the amped slugger reportedly made $2 million in endorsement fees on top of his $15.8 million salary. Back in 2001, he spawned *major* short-term deals with KFC and discount brokerage Charles Schwab. But since 1999, he's made only two long-term, enduring, big bucks endorsements—for Fila's spikes and Franklin Sports's batting gloves.

Several chastened athletes have managed to keep their sponsorship deals and recoup their public images in recent years—but these are rare and risky. Nike stood by Los Angeles Lakers guard Kobe Bryant after he was accused of rape, but Coke didn't.

There are so many examples these days that it would take extra chapters to list them all, so instead I want to concentrate on people like Jason Giambi, one man who was caught up in this bad business of steroids. In the past, he was doing many product pitches, but now no one will touch him. In December 2004, the *San Francisco Chronicle* reported that it had seen Giambi's 2003 grand jury testimony in the BALCO investigation.

The newspaper said that in his testimony, Giambi admitted to using several different steroids during the off-seasons from 2001 to 2003, and injecting himself with human growth hormone during the 2003 season. Giambi apologized publicly to the media and his fans, although he did not specifically state what for. That may have been his big mistake: he did not *really* come clean, and to this day he's a pariah. The fans hate him, so you know the advertisers do too.

Then I'm forced to discuss golfer John Daly, who was "abandoned" (his word) by sponsors and tournament organizers after he admitted that he was a chronic gambler. Then again, his anger management problem probably didn't help things much. Daly claimed he lost between $50 and $100 million during his 12-year gambling run, then took control of his life. Sadly, he never regained a golf career.

"The guy who had the incident with the bat" was slugger Sammy Sosa, who somehow made it through okay, keeping most of his $4 million endorsements from ConAgra and Pepsi, among others. Chicago Cubs outfielder Sosa first got tarnished amid allegations of his use of performance-enhancing drugs (denied), then was undercut when umpires inspecting a bat he broke found that it was plugged with cork, an illegal means of lightening bats and speeding up swings. Sosa claimed that he used the bat accidentally, and x-rays of all his other bats checked out. This lack of proof allowed Sosa to emerge okay, but he's still not on top of any list.

On-performance performance (sic) is the only thing that will let these guys get away with all that bad behavior. The bad character will go away with good play. However, let's follow the money. While the swing of the bat or the club impresses the purist fan, companies want the super-exciting, no-holds-barred superstar who spawns his own off-field hype. They want people skills—but they want good playing first.

Recall how NBA forward Dennis Rodman played with unbounded intensity on and off the basketball court. He was always doing something crazy in his love life that kept the tabs on his ass, but he had a mean layup. He is still being sued for all sorts of offenses; not sure what he hopes to get out of the publicity, but let's hope he squirreled away some cash..

Being famous means being memorable, never forget. Big corporations want characters. Buzz is about who talks about whom. That will never change. So with that . . .

The phenom that is David Beckham bends sponsors' ears because of glitz—his wife, his look, his whole façade is glitzy. How he plays is secondary. He moved to America in 2007, launched a "scent," and toyed with playing half a gay couple on *Desperate Housewives*. (His "mate" was scheduled to be soft singer Robbie Williams, who also opted against this career-defining coupledom!) But he has yet to procure major corporate riches in his new country, except inside celebrity magazines, which do not pay him—at least not yet.

The question remains: how much game does this guy still have, since no one can sustain a career on glitz alone—think Paris Hilton [will go away]. Should Beckham sit on the bench for another season, he will become the next Who Again? in sports. He'd better do superbly on the field or he will become the sporting world's biggest flameout, as his $250 million price tag affirms.

Not one sponsor will touch that game, no matter how much character he has left in him.

LYING

IS THAT YOUR FINAL ANSWER?

TREND: Lying will become fashionable again, and for starters it's become less scary to do so.

Lately it appears that everyone has forgotten the lessons of our recent forefathers (Mr. WorldCom, Mr. Rigas, and M.S. Living), and it's right back to "what can I get away with" time. Even Fox is running a game show all about really good fabricators, the retro-titled *The Moment of Truth*.

We are entering a special period where it's too easy to get caught, and that means it's scarier than ever to be a liar, since our faithful media consist of empowered citizen journalists who will do absolutely anything for a scoop—like lose sleep and not get paid. The trip down is way too swift these days.

Past years have exposed corporate greed and disdain for the consumer at its finest, Enron being the poster child. Weren't we shocked, despite our common opinion of corporate giants being anything but flattering? Remember how particularly outlandishly a few seriously shameless individuals behaved. The late Ken Lay was the face of sinister corporate evildoing. A face like ours, with a nose and eyes, but at the same time something alien. People knowingly took advantage of regular folks in ways that even 1980s players like Michael Milken could not fathom.

Afterward, people like me who write, research, teach, and practice the art of consultation were waiting for a new age of ethics. Nothing spawned, nothing earned—right?

But if you're part of the 90 percent of the world that provides service to people for a living, all you have are your good looks and your word. Why ruin either; why even exaggerate? It makes a journalist who reports the lie look like a dolt, so therefore your problems get louder and more public.

Not to mention the fabulous ethical problems.

I get the fact that people are always saying something that they quickly regret. Politicians buy back what they say every day. If this happens, if you or someone in your company lies, call back, apologize, and make some kind of amends. Say some unruly devil made you do it. But don't stand by your insolence.

It may seem obvious (it's not), but you can "get away with" telling the truth by jumping up with outside data from a third-party source—government, surveyors, or testers—that you give to the press before it starts to wonder and thereby emphasize the safety of your product or pinpoint whatever problems exist. External data are somebody else's reputation, so they're seen as cool.

As for citizen bloggers and podcasters and e-mail trend shouters, if you treat them aggressively with full disclosure, you will rebound without folks thinking, "I caught him." Use all open channels to talk about what happened, analyze what went wrong, and demonstrate how quickly you jumped!

Want proof that honesty wins any tough battle? Try Philip Morris, which has gone above and beyond a government settlement in shouting mea culpa. A firm not known to be open has been quite grassroots with its forthrightness. The company devoted resources and spoke out on TV and radio, and in blogs, chat rooms, and consumer and/or investor sites. Hollywood has taught us poorly. But it's one thing for Miss Kidman to pretend to be wed to Mr. Urban or Mr. Aiken to pretend to be a hot-blooded American lady chaser. These are performers who are paid to beguile us and sell us something that is pure fantasy! It's entirely different for a firm to bemoan a problem with statements that they and we know are pure nonsense.

Knowing that what you do passes the bullshit test and is meaningful, honest, and interesting, plus having some measure of heart, is all it takes to make it in the world of sales, marketing, PR, and all other "service" fields. If your work doesn't fit this pattern, please find something else to do.

> Informed people wish to be told what's up and are more inclined to believe those who don't pander.

So have a heart, pull the Band-Aid brand bandage off and dole out the facts. Citizens would rather laugh at Couric's travails than at your head-shaking behavior, anyway!

WE FIB

TREND: We just don't tell the truth. The smart future portends people saying, "Enough. I don't believe you."

As Dr. House will not stop saying: everybody lies! Here are corporate lies that will no longer be tolerated in *our* future:

I paid you, so I'll have to check what Accounting did.

The truth is: my board asked me to call you about this.

The investors want answers!

Of course, do it your way.

You are doing an excellent job, and I'm telling everyone.

Why would I question you, bucko?

Don't copy anyone but me on the mail. The others don't need to see it.

I mean it. You are our second choice.

Just a single change—that's it.

I *have* to cancel our agreement, sorry! The partners are the ones who are upset; it's not me. It's not you. I need to regroup. We're a mess. We are such a horrid client.

Didn't get it? Gee, it must have got caught in the network!

My bad! I can't say it was "my fault" or "I'm bad." So I joined those two.

And finally:

You really look like you lost some weight; are you on Zone?

WHY SMART SELLERS CAN SPELL FNORD

AND WHY IT REALLY MATTERS

TREND: Turn on customers with what's unsaid loudly between the lines. (2011, not to be too self-referential, is filled with line hiders!)

There's a guy named Robert Anton Wilson, a writer whom people who think about trends a lot talk about—a lot. Wilson, who was first an editor at *Playboy* after a terrible bout of childhood polio, is a cult unto himself. But in the 1960s and 1970s, a series of life-changing moments turned him into a real thinker and an intelligence agent!

His books were known as conspiracies, rock festivals, filled with vivid images and real connections to our world, written as though submerged under water in a blue field of misnomers, guides to what's beneath the surface, and of course metaphors for us to learn about. Wilson at first was so darn poor as a writer (no one would publish his stuff for a long while) that his family lived on welfare while he struggled to see his dream through to fruition.

And if you wonder why he was such a conspiracy freak, you have to wade through his book series titled *Illuminatus!* (the exclamation point is urgent), in which he unearths a secret society within a secret story that could still exist to forge world powers.

Well, anyway, in this amazing man's book series, written with friend and writer Bob Shea, Wilson talks about a concept that I happen to be really into: it is called Fnord. Fnords are mythological creatures who reside between the lines of text. Fnords are brilliant and scary. Fnords are pretty hard to explain.

I could go on and on. Fnord is important to our present and our future. It is "representation of disinformation or irrelevant information intending to misdirect." That's from the user-friendly encyclopedia site Answers.com, which has a habit of getting right to the point, even when certain authors don't. The word was popularized by the *Illuminatus!* trilogy—yes, the book comes in three parts. But what Wilson fans love is that all great artists drop what they're doing and lose their place—some of the meanings of Fnord are lost because the author actually lost them. Wilson was so popular in his day that he collected definitions of his made-up words and shared these Spock-lock with his legions, but in the end much of his stuff was thrown out.

What happened to the lost Fnord descriptions was that Wilson cut 500 pages of the book to please his publisher (go figure), and so he forgot what he was talking about. I tend to forget what I mean to say too, but for far different reasons.

Yet in each of the three novels, Wilson speaks of the Fnord in the words we use, words that have been given hypnotic power over those whom he called "the unenlightened." In the first volume of *Illuminatus!*—a strange and really challenging book (but not challenging in the way Dostoyevsky is)—actual kids in grade school were not able to consciously see the word *Fnord.* For the rest of the kids' lives, said Wilson in these works, appearances of the word subconsciously generated a feeling of unease and confusion and prevented rational consideration of the subject. So in that 900-page opus, Fnords are everywhere.

The word *Fnord* first sprang from the subcultural movement of Discordianism back in the 1960s, appearing within the pages of the *Principia Discordia*, written in 1965 by Greg Hill (a.k.a. Malaclypse the Younger) and Kerry Thornley (a.k.a. Omar Khayyam Ravenhurst). While initially depicted as a bit of pseudo-Zen gibberish in Discordian circles, Fnord took on a more sophisticated connotation when used in Shea and Anton Wilson's classics, particularly one I read on my new Kindle (plug nice, right, Amazon?), *The Golden Apple*.

Within the context of Shea and Wilson's work, Fnord evolved beyond nonsense-laden origins, becoming a neurolinguistic component within a totalitarian control system. Fancy, eh! Sprinkled within the text of mass media publications, such Fnords were used as a means to subliminally trigger a subconscious sense of dread within the populace, imposing control via a subtext of fear.

Understandably, Fnord took on a distinctly conspiratorial bent in Shea and Wilson's stories. However, once Shea and Wilson popularized the term in their novels, the applicability and use of Fnord expanded further.

Though Shea and Wilson had depicted Fnord as a typographic device designed to exclusively instill fear, this has blurred over time as the connotations surrounding Fnord have grown in number and degrees of abstraction. By today's most basic definition, Fnord—now a symbol as much as a word—signifies any veiled attempt at coercion. Thus, to "see the fnords" means that one is cognizant of this, seeing past the ruse.

However, Wilson said outright that there are no *real* Fnords in advertising, encouraging a consumer society. What's fascinating is that Fnord in a newspaper or magazine causes fear and anxiety concerning current events. In *Illuminatus!* Fnord is not the word *used* but a substitute, since readers cannot see the actual word. That needs a few rereadings. Work for your knowledge.

According to Eric Wagner, whose writings on Wilson are huge in Fnordish circles, when you "note a Fnord," it refers to a major breakthrough in a novel by characters who are attempting to gain control of their nervous systems.

Yeah I know. It's confusing. Bear with me. It's worth the wait.

Fnord is the stuff between words—where we hide all the intention. It's what's left unsaid. Like when a car salesperson murmurs, "Buy this hot sports car!" what he's really saying is that it will get you laid and that unless you're behind the wheel of this car, you're not special.

Fnord is what you hear behind the scenes when a Southern lady says "That's nice!" and really means "Go fuck yourself."

Though all of that is left unspoken, it's still highly effective on a subconscious level.

I see one variety of Diet Coke has a new vitamin version— pure Fnord. This brand extension is wholeheartedly about the fact that no school would *ever* take Coke out of the vending machines. But this is a way for parents not to hate them. It's all within the words "Resolve to be better with great taste."

A friend and I used to bat around a phrase mocking all the unspoken intentions within political rhetoric and advertising: "You don't say?!"

Whenever anyone was bullshitting us, we'd just nod emphatically and say, "Fnord." Kind of like "fighting fire with fire," but perhaps we were "fighting Fnord with Fnord." I don't know how effective this was, but it was worth a few laughs at least!

So what is Fnord, then?

"Fnord is that funny feeling you get when you reach for the Snickers bar and come back holding a Slurpee."

Or:

Fnord is the bucket where they keep the unused serifs for H*lvetica.

Fnord is the gunk that sticks to the inside of your car's fenders.

Fnord is the source of all the zero bits in your computer."

Above is from Fnord.com. I have my own, but for those see Laermer.com/whatmeans.

The site as always makes it better, or at least easier to cope with: Fnord.org/occult/discordia/text/what.is.Fnord. (I have a pet peeve about printed media that toss in heady URLs for readers, and I promise that everything mentioned that's Web-searchable is on Laermer.com so you don't think I'm as big a hypocrite as I do.)

May I just say—before closing snappily—that in entertainment, when a star agrees to do an interview with a reporter, he or she is usually doing so with the absolute understanding that what he or she says is discussed as news, even though, in most cases, they could rip him or her to shreds, they being the "media." Fnords are huge in that regard.

And now one bit worth riffing on from Wikipedia: in the also-ran movie *They Live*, the main character discovers a similar conspiracy when hidden conformity messages start appearing on billboards, magazines, TV, and currency that are revealed only to those wearing special sunglasses. To see Fnord means to be unaffected by the supposed hypnotic power of the word or, more loosely, of other fighting words. The phrase "I have seen Fnords" was graffitied on a railway crossing, known as Anarchy Bridge, located in the City Center between Earlston and Coventry in the United Kingdom until the 1990s, when the old bridge was replaced. The bridge and the phrase were mentioned in the novel *A Touch of Love* by Jonathan Coe.

It is often used to indicate a random or surreal sentence.

Fnord is an apostrophe on drugs.

Fnord is the gunk that sticks to the inside of your car's fenders.

Fnord is the source of all the zero bits in your computer.

Is this chapter jarringly out of context? That in itself is Fnord. According to many, Fnord is an actual meaning of life. Say, is *Fnord* simply "dog spelled backwards"? Think about it: it is a word inside another term. It's spooky but believable.

Oh, and since thus far I have not been able to get you to believe that Fnord is at all crucial to your own life, let's just say . . .

Fnord and/or Laermer.com/whatishedoingonpage81.

Yes—Sadly—Sprint Was Correct

TREND: When your customers are horrible to you in every conceivable way, you will drop them. Bad publicity will not stop you from doing it. People will see that your behavior is right.

In mid-2007, Sprint sent about a thousand subscribers scrambling for a new wireless carrier because of their excessive customer service use. They actually shut these people up by saying, "Go away, we hate you." Rivals are making hay with the action by declaring that they'd never ever drop customers. But, if you think about it, Sprint made the right move. Here are the lessons you should learn.

Not all customers are alike. In fact, there are such things as good and bad customers. Good customers use your goods and services at a rate that provides reasonable revenue. Bad customers make demands and consume resources; they don't care about conflict resolution, and they cost the company big bucks.

Sprint says that its average subscriber calls customer service about once a month, mostly for billing and technical support issues. The dropped customers were calling CS 40 to 50 times each month, many times with problems that Sprint had nothing to do with. For example, they wanted information about other subscribers' accounts! Read between the lines: Sprint believed there was nothing it could do to satisfy them.

So Sprint said, "Go away. Leave us alone. Don't ever even listen to a *pin drop* again!" Here I realize I'm going back, oh, about five years ago, when Sprint—now Sprint-Nextel—said that its phone lines were so clear you could hear a pin drop. Whatever . . . I'm old. When you consider that Sprint has 54 million subscribers, the idea of a handful of problem customers causing headaches may be a bit outlandish. The reality is, these subscribers were not only chewing up resources but denying other subscribers access to deal with legitimate problems.

Companies are dumb if they look at customers as being equal in terms of sales and revenue potential. In other words, if they're willing to buy, we are willing to sell. Two customers with the same order with the same cost and margin structure won't always provide the same revenue because no two customers are alike in their expectations or their demand for services.

Companies must qualify prospects before converting them to so-called customers or risk taking on unwanted problem accounts that will drain resources and make for opportunity losses.

Think about it. (Or don't; it's your choice.) When a few of your clients start calling for help, demanding faster response times and making excessive requests for special services, they consume the bandwidth that's supposed to be servicing the base. Support overload spreads to the sales and back office, too, since these customers are likely to demand more face time and follow-up from sales reps, account managers, and

Accounting, not to mention the high-level mucky-mucks that have to hear about them constantly.

Like you, I've been mad at Sprint for years because of its subacceptable customer service, I've reserved heyweretrying.com for when they decide to cut that shit out. but it does have a right to stop people from abusing its people and, particularly, being unreasonable. As a business owner, I applaud Sprint. As a customer, I've secretly switched to Verizon. Okay, okay, to be fair, the Sprint Hi-Speed Wireless service is gorgeous and works seamlessly, but the branding on its card drives me insane (whose is it? Novatel's?).

FRITO-LAY'S CHOLESTEROL STORY

TREND: The more some company says something's good for us, the sooner we'll be suspicious.

"This generation may be the first one not to live longer than their parents' generation. Frito-Lay wants to play a part in stopping this from happening," said David Rader, executive vice president of Frito-Lay, in a moment of chutzpah that may outlive us all.

Frito-Lay is raising eyebrows along with our nervous energy as it markets itself as the supplier of the nutritionally savvy person's junk food of choice. In January 2007, the company—makers of Cheetos, Doritos, and other key components of any healthy diet—notified the Food and Drug Administration of its intention to capitalize on provisions in the FDA Modernization Act that allow manufacturers to integrate into their labels health claims that are grounded in "authoritative scientific study." The chipmaker wished to highlight the relationship between the replacement of saturated fats with unsaturated fatty acids and a reduced risk of heart disease on many of its products. In May 2007, the FDA agreed to allow the snack food giant to print the following modified language:

> Replacing saturated fat with similar amounts of unsaturated fats may reduce the risk of heart disease. To achieve this benefit, total daily calories should not increase.

The new labeling is only one part of Frito-Lay's strategy to win over consumers by styling itself as a purveyor of health-conscious snacks. The company introduced Natural Cheetos with organic corn in 2003, and began making Tostitos and Doritos with corn oil at around the same time. In 2004 the company introduced Rolled Gold heart-shaped pretzels in the United States (yuckily dubbed "Heartzels") in partnership with the American Heart Association, in what Frito-Lay described as the latest example of "its commitment to offering a wide variety of low-fat and better-for-you snacks," and in 2006 the company's switch to NuSun sunflower oil in many of its products was accompanied by packaging that married the iconic Lay's logo with a sunflower. Frito-Lay's PepsiCo corporate parent has put its "Smart Spot" label on nearly 300 products that meet the company's own nutritional standards (these can include products with a "functional benefit," such as hydration).

What does all this mean? In a twenty-first-century America fraught with childhood obesity, a rising occurrence of diabetes, and growing public nutritional awareness, Frito-Lay's petitioning of the FDA for Heart Healthy labeling represents a careful and I say obnoxious attempt to stay ahead in a snack foods industry that generates more than $10 billion annually.

During a Q1 2007 earnings conference call for corporate parent PepsiCo, one executive explained that across the Frito-Lay and Quaker food businesses, a major goal was to "drive premium health and wellness innovation." A centerpiece of this approach was to be the "healthy" SunChips brand, which had seen revenues soar. But they're greasy, and when I eat them on airplanes, crumbs soil my shirt. How can this be healthy?

To complement SunChips, PepsiCo has also introduced the Flat Earth brand, which executives praise as being healthy even without proof of concept. Sales and consumer acceptance of snacks such as Granola Bites, Baked Muffin Bars, and Mini Delights are supposed to be healthy, but no one can say with what ingredients.

While a newfound emphasis on nutritional value is admirably profitable, observers are becoming skeptical of Frito-Lay's new marketing spin and have attacked the "Heart Healthy" label as misleading. As my favorite food center, The Diet Blog, argues, "The trouble with such health claims is that a single nutrient is taken out of context." A snack made mostly of refined grains, added sugars, and vegetable oil (as Frito-Lay favorites are) "is hardly a healthy product."

In January 2005 the Institutes of Medicine group, which serves as an advisory body for the government, hosted a Workshop on Marketing Strategies That Foster Healthy Food and Beverage Choices in Children and Youth. The event featured speakers from conglomerates such as Kraft, PepsiCo, and McDonald's. It was reported that health advocates had almost no representation.

A parody headline from the ONION, "Frito-Lay Angrily Introduces New Line of Healthy Snacks," succinctly captures my own reaction to Frito-Lay's real-life product rollout: that any healthy alternatives proposed by this multiconglomerate represent nothing more than cynical posturing aimed at boosting the bottom line, consumer health be damned.

How to Major in Napping

TREND: Let's get some sleep—and get *beaucoup* money.

When I was in my twenties, I befriended Marge Champion, the dancer who in *her* twenties was married to choreographer Gower Champion. Together, they formed a famous Boy and Girl Next Door–type couple who hoofed it up on Broadway and in movies, then, like most all-American couples, divorced. Marge went on to be a beloved dancer and step-maker, and we met when she was in her late sixties; I marveled at how she worked her hoofs off.

"Nap, dear, every single day. Take half an hour at around 4 o'clock every day and split those days into two! It's the only way."

But alas, sleep has its detractors, my father being one of them. In my teen years, he got on my case about how much sleep I was getting—and I am a nap aficionado. To him it was always too much! "You snooze, you lose," was his tossed bon mot. I took his words to heart, while in my head thinking that sleep was the ultimate source of creativity and inspiration.

I found I was not alone in feeling this way. As I grew older, I stopped listening to my father and started getting ideas from pop. I learned that "Yesterday" came to McCartney in a dream and that the very inspiration behind Richards's riffing on "(I Can't Get No) Satisfaction" was out of a snoozefest.

Like many of my friends, I discovered that authors and scientists make these claims too, and I'm sure most of it's lore (ask me about "Torn between Two Lovers" being recorded in a bathroom!). Probably the best-known claims come from Samuel Coleridge, with his sleep-inspired poem "Kubla Khan" ("A Vision in a Dream"), and Nobelist Otto Loewi, who insisted that his chemical theory of neurotransmission was a dream sequence like the one from *Dallas*, only more believable.

This notion that more goes on in our sleep than just rest has captivated science fiction writers for nearly the last 100 years. And a number of writers have speculated about ways in which humanity could use sleep to learn. One of the earliest literary references to sleep learning was in Hugo Gernsback's 1911 novel *Ralph 124c41+: A Romance of the Year 2660*, in which the author describes a device called a Hypnobioscope that was designed to embed information in the sleeper's mind. While Gernsback's depiction may have come first, Aldous Huxley's depiction of sleep learning in *Brave New World* is the one most of us got wind of in college.

Some scientists were apparently intrigued enough by these literary depictions that they decided to investigate for themselves. Initial studies into sleep learning's success, back in the 1940s and 1950s, were supportive of the theory that people could in fact learn in their sleep. But whether this benefited the student was debatable. The value of the knowledge retained, closely akin to rote memorization, was limited, since sleep learning did not allow the subjects to ascertain the relevance or context of the information they were supposedly learning.

Despite the initial promise of sleep learning, the general consensus in the scientific community is that the talked-about research is outdated. However, the same collective seems to be taking another look at sleep now. And there is a trend that is currently on the rise to focus on utilizing sleep for more than just catching Zs. Contrary to Dad's well-worn advice, sleeping can be quite productive both during and after your time away from waking consciousness.

Scientists have begun to discover how essential sleeping is to creativity and problem solving. According to a German study sponsored by the University of Luebeck that appeared in the journal *Nature*: "Pivotal insights can be gained through sleep. . . . It consolidates memories and, concomitantly, could allow insight by changing their representational structure." This study also showed that when presented with a basic math test, subjects who had had a full eight hours of sleep were three times more likely than sleep-deprived participants to solve a puzzle embedded in the test.

And a Harvard Medical School study came to the conclusion that "a night of sleep after being exposed to a class of mathematical problems more than doubles the likelihood of discovering" a solution.

And whereas sleep learning offered only the promise of our being able to regurgitate information from the night before, our latest understanding of sleep tells us that it is instrumental in the processing of memory and is vital to insight. A study from the University of Luebeck that we talked about already showed that a particularly important period of deep sleep called slow-wave sleep (SWS) is involved in the restructuring of memories from the previous day. This restructuring was linked to an increase in brainpower. Since SWS is one of the deepest parts of our internal sleep cycle, you can understand why it's important to get a full night's sleep.

We are already accustomed to sleep aids like Ambien and Lunesta that are intended to make sure we get the sleep we need, although they really only make us drowsy enough to do the work ourselves. We are in debt to these drug wonders when our fists are clenched at night, but we're now beginning to see products intended for more than just that. There's a weight-loss product that actually works while we sleep now—though the much-advertised thought of something oozing from my behind makes me queasy.

Some sleepy-time devices, like the Hemi-Sync CD, are marketed as a "way to boost cognitive power by enhancing your sleep experience. Monroe Institute Hemi-Sync CDs for children help their young listeners learn more, retain more, concentrate, relax, and sleep. Hemi-Sync is a safe and effective way to maximize your child's potential."

But Hemi-Sync is just the beginning. In April of 2007, psychiatrist Giulio Tononi and his colleagues at the University of Wisconsin–Madison utilized a procedure called transcranial magnetic stimulation (TMS) to stimulate SWS in participants, which is a fancy way of saying that they strapped magnets to volunteers' heads to see if this helped bring SWS on. More important, Tononi was quoted saying: "With a single pulse, we were able to induce a wave that looks identical to the waves the brain makes normally during sleep."

There is further speculation that TMS sleep applications could be implemented to confer a magnetically induced power nap where you could get the equivalent of eight hours sleep in a fraction of the time. Imagine—more time to do what?

So magnetic sleep helmets are coming, and sooner than you think, since there are other devices like the Kvasar Dreammask or Novadreamer lucid dreaming inducer already on the market, as well as the Morpheus REM monitor—all of which are designed to enhance your experience in bed. No, not that experience . . . !

> Once it dawns upon the powers that be just how much impact sleep has on the bottom line, we all might be demanded to get more shut-eye.

However, while creativity has long been associated with productivity, it remains to be seen just how long it will take for corporate America to become fully aware of the connection between sleep, creativity, and a potentially tremendous boost to the productivity of their knowledge base. But there are encouraging signs in the realm of work safety that seem to hint at a sea change on the horizon.

Employers realize the necessity of things like naps at work (my own firm built a "nap space" in the go-go 1990s, way before a Nap Center was installed in the Empire State Building) in order to keep creativity and retention moving. I hear that machine shops ask people to nap to prevent them from being prone to accidents! And you better believe that there's already a device to help you take that nap you always want around 3 p.m. Though the makers score no points for the originality of their product name, the PowerNap NapMachine, which I covet daily, promises "3 hours of deep sleep in 20 minutes" (powernap.com).

It's only a matter of time before the prevailing perspective shifts from reactive and safety-oriented to proactive sleep enhancement and all the creative benefits that obviously accrue from it. Hopefully, we won't wait too long for that to change. Judging by the bags under the eyes of bugged-out executives these days, maybe everyone has to sleep on it.

One way or another, let's stay awake to see what happens.

e. e. cummings would freak

October 22, 2007

Dear You Who Made It This Far:

Yep, it sure does appear that everyone wants to be cute with their monikers these days. Didn't anyone learn from those disastrous dot-com companies? Being adorable means nothing and does not translate into sales. But I see falling by the wayside the cruddy use of lowercase letters, like when Biography Channel calls itself "bio." or Court TV, "truTV" (a misnomer if ever there was one). Or when a lame catalog company dubs itself "smith + hawken" (what's wrong with "and," anyway?).

And when the new performers need to think like "k.d. lang" and use teeny letters to make a statement, I shudder to think that they believe we care. I know true (tru?) genius can do whatever it wants, but we've yet to see any from the likes of the brand called "altogether."

There is a band called lower case a (myspace.com/lowercasea), and it's pretty good, but still derivative.

I stop and inform you that, just as in all the fake retirement ploys and Simple Is as Simple Does branding, the next decade will be refreshingly, shockingly devoid of those who use lettering to make a name for themselves.

There is also going to be the evolutionary ceasing of ScrunchedTogether style, like, well, everything: LiveSearch, MySpace, YouTube, TrendSpotting (2002), EnoughAlready! Gees.

The truth is, it's high time to rid ourselves of adorability. We all knew when we were dotcomologists that it was important to follow *that* trend of words that had middle letters capitalized. Now just say your name— spell it out without irony. Two words if it's two. Three if it's three. One if it's one . . . and (sic) no more lowercase laziness.

With love,

r

WELCOME TO BAS

I'M TALKING TO YOU

TREND: The end of bait and switch in corporations.

I'd like to imagine that somewhere, at some college or university, there's a lecture being held called "No More Bait and Switch." With that fantasy in my head, I bring you . . . that class.

In many respects nothing changes, and I mean never. For instance, I've been watching service businesses pull some serious crap for years. No matter what happens, the practice of bait and switch (BAS) still persists. After downturns, the price of coffee skyrocketing, the freaking mortgage collapse, terrorism, wars, famine, pestilence (okay, not that), and Katrina, firms still sell people to new clients and have them disappear once the so-called ink is good and dry.

BAS is what happens when people come to a meeting with you to sell a service and then run away after the agreement is filed and the work begins. It's offensive. Facetious charm and canny fanciness are replaced by bargain youth. Not that there's anything wrong with young people. It's just not who was being proffered as the doer of deeds. Every now and then I'll meet an executive who says to me, "Who actually does the work at your place?"

Then the flashback music plays and I start to consider. Hmm. I guess the trend here is that *that* always seems to be changing. In every firm that offers a service, you can't simply decide who will handle your needed duties on a daily basis. You have to be flexible. Please remember that anyone who's being paid could jump at any time. These days, people often don't show up for work because of the sniffles, and they sometimes leave because their boss didn't phone at home to say "Attaboy!" And yet every single fucking day *someone* has to do the actual servicing of customers.

That means it kind of has to be the larger-than-life folks who sold the service in the first place! And the folks being sold to simply are for a fact not stupid, so why not make it easier for people and say who will do the work? In nearly every "new business" meeting I've gone to, someone is folding her arms thinking: "Who is this guy? Will I ever see this smart aleck again? Is anyone here as fabulous as he is (aww)?"

And as for the reasons why companies do this—there's only one: because it's cheaper, that's why. Why should the stars get their hands dirty? Purell smells. It's so much more fun to pontificate and strategize and make up hyphenated terms . . . and get out of the office at a reasonable hour. Plus (insert evil laugh) they get to boss folks around. What utter coolness! In an effort to slow the BS that happens every day, here are some tough questions to ask slick sales guys:

- What percentage of the business will you, oh fancy speaker, do for me?

- How many assignments do you work on for real? Who else would be involved in this? May I meet them?

- How many hours do you spend on non-sales-like-work?

- Who does the research, and can analyze it and counsel me and talk to me like I'm the Man?

- Who reports to me on what's up?

- Who's my day-to-day? Give me his home number.

- Do you actually come to work every gosh-darn day?

- Have you always been so flashy? (Ask him where he got the tie, or where she got that beaded broach.)

   Sure, there are people who can do high-level sales and keep their humility in order to be worker bee. There are some folks who are awesome at both, G-d love 'em. But it's a rarity, and BAS is the norm. Follow the above advice and get what you paid for. Oh, and if you get handed off to someone named Tiffany, my advice is run. No walking.

> Most salespeople are smiling fancy-pants types, and your daily contacts are usually raw at best.

   Go to Laermer.com/bas for a quiz on whether you have been baited and switched—and like *Cosmo*, whether you can get out of that unhealthy relationship!

GREET THIS

HOW A CITY CIVILITY CAMPAIGN RUINED FRIENDLINESS

TREND: Let's stop being so plastic, and push for a lack of sameness in the place we call home. Less a trend; more a plea.

U p until the mid 1990s, the City of New York, my birthplace, had very restrictive zoning laws that limited the number of chain stores that could set up shop in any given neighborhood. Thus, people who grew up in New York were unfamiliar with such all-American delicacies as Taco Bell (as compared to, say, a Jamaican patty) and could never distinguish between Dunkin' Donuts and Krispy Kreme, but they all talked endlessly about Harlem's own Georgie's Pastry Shop (voted best donut on earth in the *New York Times* before it closed because of a landlord's usurious behavior—damn him!).

When people visited New York, you could see the confusion flicker in their eyes. They'd never heard of any of these places. Where to eat? Sal's? Tony's? Kennedy Fried Chicken? Service was often New York rude—Whaddaya want?—until you knew the guy who ran the place. But you *could* get to know him, since he was probably there every day. Now we've got a Domino's in every neighborhood. And if you don't like the pizza . . . well, tough. New York coffee was terrible, but it cost 60 cents and it was *New York* coffee. There were cafes you could go to "in the Village," and they were superb. But that was for special occasions.

Why did the city trade its unique character in exchange for a series of urban mini-malls along the "former Ladies Mile" of Sixth Avenue and around the infamous area known as Union Square, where soapbox politicians once shouted for big weekend crowds? Gee, money! What am I always telling you?

Why shop at five mom-and-pop stores when you can get everything you want at the Bed and Bath Superstore? And the city got big tax payoffs for letting the big companies move in. Plus the big stores moved into areas that were considered rundown by the city (which often meant that they were the cheapest places to shop). So now we've got a Kmart and not one but two Starbucks sitting on artsy Astor Square. If you think I'm screaming for nothing, let me tell you that *even* Barnes & Noble had to vamoose from Astor because the rent was too expensive!

What you get in these places is often fewer options, longer lines, and higher prices in exchange for the convenience of one-stop shopping. And you get Blockbuster employees being forced to call you by your first name (its ridiculous company policy) instead of someone who actually knows you.

"46"

THE MIDDLE AGES

TREND: The creators of products and services that allow us to live better will win out over creators of those that make us live **longer.**

So I write this chapter on the day of my forty-sixth birthday, which is half the age my grandfather was when he passed away at an unimaginable (to me) 92 years.

It's at this point that I realize, without much effort, how much life begins when you really stop thinking about the stuff you didn't do and concentrate on what's ahead.

The next decade, the one that rises above mediocrity, will be one where people begin to count not their blessings per se, but the wonder of it all: and this is not a Jetsonian wonder at the coolness of all the stuff at our fingertips, literally, but more one that says, heck, it's amazing we're even still around what with all the fighting and calamity that we stare at on our computer screens.

Oh, and forget this crap about the older years being the time to celebrate life, anyway.

And sure, I know that if you're under 30, you're desperately seeking the next section of this book, but hold on.

I am not 50 yet, and yet I shake my head at the 50-plus and AARP set that wants people like me to think we're about to enter some *Golden Girls* set. As Woody Allen said in a moment of unscripted brilliance: "I just don't see any advantage in getting older. It's not like you suddenly get wise and accept the world for what it is, accept people for what they are, and suddenly realize what love is—none of that happens."

A few years ago I went to a conference run by financier/bald guy Michael Milken, and he talked about the future being "huge" for products to help us live longer lives. It occurred to me that Milken was a different (read: way older) generation from me and was darkly foretelling a curtain coming down on his rich self. For me and mine, it's not really about going way far into the future; we know that what Allen said about the tragedy of it all is true. It doesn't matter how chipper we act day to day; we're facing an uphill climb that we did to ourselves by living well.

Here's a fact to consider: products or services that make *our* lives sweet and fabulous will do a lot better than those that keep *our* selfish asses alive longer. When I asked my grandmother about living as long as she did (87), her response stayed with me for a long time: "I'm just waiting."

Waiting sounds gauche. I'd like those foods that make me feel fit, the crèmes that soften my face, new clothing I don't have to wash a lot, and of course to be treated like a sage old guy who is more special than decrepit.

Stop with all the mirrors being sold in every possible fashion—our generation isn't as excited to see ourselves all the time as the last one was. We can dress ourselves in the morning and move on. As Courtney Cox muttered while promoting, I'm sure, face cream: "I definitely have issues with getting old! There are huge changes in my body and face lately. I just try not to have too many mirrors around."

On a serious note: I queried my pals on the first day of year 46. They, like me, want to wait it out in some luxury and a hell of a good-looking state, so, uh, dude, if you're a trendsetting entrepreneur with ideas up your sleeve, I sincerely hope you are planning to help me out here.

The New Low in Business Etiquette

Stealing without Aplomb

TREND: The age of form letters will be replaced by one in which no matter what we do, we use style and gusto. Even when we're being oblique.

Like you, everything I do is personal. But when folks start ripping off business from me and making my industry look bad by the manner in which the thievery is committed, I decide to take action.

Here, then, is a dissertation on being stolen from by someone lower on the food chain.

It's okay to steal biz, because everyone gets the urge to eat the lunch of a competitor. But doing it in a way that makes everyone look tawdry and insignificant brings us all down.

One lady from Biz Dev at another PR firm asked a client of mine, a known CEO of an upstart tech firm, for his money. But in doing so, she used a form letter with no couth, details, ideas, or imagination, and so the CEO wrote her and me to say that it was the worst letter he'd ever gotten: poorly written, devoid of ideas, and particularly trite, without research or backup. He even used a word that made me flinch: generic.

Talk about busted.

Oh and let me tell you *how she did it*:

> I recently noticed some news on your company which caught my eye. I apologize for the impersonal e-mail, but I want to introduce you to my firm. [Full names are left in to hurt the criminal—see Laermer.com for more.] . . . We have been in business for over 20 years and are creative in spinning our clients' stories to the media. . . . If you would like to hear some of our PR ideas, I can contact you. For more information about . . . please visit our Web site.

Did you laugh at "I can contact you"? It's like please do me a big favor, as if my client doesn't get a letter like this one once a week at least. Drop everything and respond because you are the PR love of my life.

Whatever.

This gal embarrassed the two of us *and* our mutual profession with such a ham-fisted approach to doing me in. Here's the overriding question: why is *everything* just tossed off these days? Whether it's lazy e-mails or vapid communication or CYA to clients ("Sounds good!" "I'm with you!") or the letters we send to prospects like this poopy-head above, it's as if we're playing a game of numbers instead of putting thought onto the monitor.

Are we so busy that we simply want to "git 'er done" instead of putting in the real mental energy? Have approach and grammar become so damn unimportant in these fast-paced, vowel-dropping, texted-to-death times of ours?

In service businesses, the latest scheme run amok is our letting technology override how we target the communications we send out: with our heads and not our hands.

If it's all form and formality, then what good is the communication? Let's just get Hal (dastardly machine in Kubrick's 2001), because I know he's not working! Besides, if you start a relationship with a form letter, how will you ever get her phone number?

The BD person in question swore that she didn't know my client had public relations representation. Alas, when she looked up the CEO's e-mail on his site, she could just as easily have clicked on Press Contact and figured this out. But it bugs me more that someone outside the agency saw the crud being filed by my peers, and so this CEO-for-life type will think twice before letting "people like me" at his boardroom table in the near future.

It comes down to elegance, style, and caring. To send a letter that you would delete on first glance shows clueless behavior put forth by consequence-forgetting folks, and worse, someone who claims to be representing her firm as a developer of new clientele!

It's harder than ever to get through to anyone with our own carefully chosen words—and isn't the idea to put thought into the messages sent out, regardless of who, what, or where?

VICTORIA'S SECRET'S MENTALITY

How Cities Got Overtaken by Lingerie

TREND: The coming move toward making our kids better citizens will be first to teach them that making tons of money devising crud for the masses is no way to succeed.

I'm not yet convinced that global warming will be the end for our beings, but I do have a nonwishbone to pick with celebrated rich folks like Laurie David who won't stop saying this is what will destroy our kids. People talk ad infinitum about leaving a cleaner and visibly unaffected air, land, and sea for our offspring. But what about leaving them less of a "sell-out" world?

I see a future (I'd like to stop it) being run by Victoria's Secret fans, people whose business model is shameful and one that says to the world: quality is not the issue—sales are.

Victoria's Secret sells what amounts to a rather less-than-high-quality product at a decent price. But the whole idea of buying something at less than you expect is that it doesn't last long. Cheap and value-priced are not the same.

I get it. Every girl/woman in America wants to feel sexy, but she won't necessarily buy lingerie from higher-up venues like, for instance, department stores. She will shop at a local venue, surely, and that's why in many cities, the corner supermarket has been replaced by a multitude of VS locations.

A synopsis I garnered of working conditions for Victoria's Secret workers throughout the world is that they have a routine shift of around 15 hours a day, seven days a week, creating the "stuff" that is made by poor people and for which women in other tax brackets pay to appear sexy in.

News sources tell me that workers are paid less than 50 cents an hour and are not paid for overtime. One overseas workshop of sewers was forced into what Americans might call "involuntary servitude"—all in the guise of creating undergarments. Granted, Wal-Mart, Target, and The Limited do the same, but there's something uncanny about the types of items we are asking people to buy in the case of Victoria's Secret.

When you walk through cities in the world now, there are many teeny family-run shops selling higher-quality teddies and see-through straplesses, but what they don't have is the catalog business of a Victoria's Secret.

First, this company is cutting virgin forests to print these catalogs, which is not only immoral but sounds bad (virgins!). Victoria's Secret mails out 395 million catalogs a year—more than one million every day—printed on paper made from some of the world's last remaining endangered forests. Another strike.

Victoria's Secret isn't so interested in full exposure when it comes to revealing where its catalogs come from. The paper is Canadian Boreal brand from a forest wilderness larger than the Brazilian Amazon that is being "clear cut" (totally ripped down) at a rate of two acres a minute, 24 hours a day, mainly for paper that shows off cheaply clad models grinning for our use.

- Approximately 395 million catalogs are mailed out by Victoria's Secret each year—that's more than one million a day.

- Most of these catalogs end up in the trash or recycling—often without even being looked at.

- Almost all of these catalogs are produced from fiber paper with little or no recycled content.

- Making the paper for these catalogs is destroying forests, some might say needlessly

- Victoria's Secret is not satisfied with just stripping the Boreal; it is also destroying forests in the southern United States. These forests are among the most biologically diverse regions of our country, and nearly six million acres of forest are logged each year, primarily for the production of paper. And not even something useful, like toilet style.

I rest my case with this collection of juicy facts. But let's say VS has won the war—until those who protest for a living take their aim at those corporate entities selling crap in the worst way possible.

Was it worth it for the people involved in creating this fake need? And what does it say when major towns don't turn around and tell the Secretives: "Enough. We need to have some stores in these neighborhoods that aren't merely bras and panties."

The saddest part of the story is that nothing was good enough for its founder, Roy Raymond, who sold the chain in 1982 to Limited, the Columbus, Ohio–based chain of derivative Gap-like clothing, after just a few years.

Raymond was a lingerie guy and a business leader of a sort. I read how he felt embarrassed trying to purchase lingerie for his wife (who later divorced him) in the very public and awkward department store environment, so, like a lot of later

Internet entrepreneurs, he decided to open something for people like him, and he did so in a mall near his alma mater, Stanford.

In 1993, after several failed attempts to start a new business, he committed suicide from the Golden Gate Bridge. He was 47 and was wearing underwear.

Fred Trump and That Other Guy

TREND: People like The Donald will be hoist by their own petard (kids, look up the phrase on Ask.com—or just ask).

I am a big fan of Fred C. Trump, father of that other guy. The elder Trump, the way I hear it, stood for something—a self-made real estate billionaire who, unlike his slicker, stranger, galling son, was low-key and possessed little ego. He originated my favorite business saying: You don't get anything done in the office. Phew.

Hard-working, paternal, and sincere, he took credit only for what he did. But the son, alas, fell pretty far from this tree, to mangle a metaphor.

Born and raised in Queens, Fred Trump knew from an early age that he wanted to work with his hands. His wish was carpentry, but when he was 11, his father died, and he had to help support his mother and a younger brother by working in a local fruit store 12 hours a day for $5 a week. He graduated from high school in 1922 and eventually formed his own home construction company, in partnership with his older sister. His mother had to sign the legal papers because he was just 17. From this modest beginning, he went on to build one of the most substantial real estate empires in the United States, later managing more than 25,000 apartment units, most of which he built himself, during an illustrious career spanning more than 70 years.

The story the family tells about Poppa Trump is that he was a Horatio Alger hero, a man who built himself up from nothing during the Depression. In fact, his own father, Fred Trump, Sr., was a builder who left a sizable estate, some $30,000. Still, young Fred worked as if he had nothing. He taught his children to work hard, too.

And in the near future, all the odds are against the DTs' (Donald and his ilk, or people who scream about their wonderful selves when the truth belies these fallacies) getting us to admire them or pay them heed. Trumpism means admiring someone who wants us to believe he is an icon when in fact he is a well-worn poseur and a creep.

For those of us generally thought of as egotists, Donald J. Trump is an icon for the mediocrity decade. The Don has been celebrated purely for his ability to make noise.

With the confidence of an army, and a pretty gross one, it was only a matter of time before he became the latest thing to make noise in reality television, which to those of us who remember them is very much like those "900" porn lines of the early 1990s.

Trump isn't all he's cracked up to be, so let's do a reality TV check on what his newfound fame has wrought. I saw half *The Apprentice* once, and it was neither entertaining nor compelling nor enlightening. Give something away on television? Not new. Ben Stein earned money and doled it out to contestants who answered some goofily intelligent questions with a wink and a nod. It was good TV—and pretty sensible too.

But America, and then the rest of the world, got Trumped by *The Apprentice*, and the man took many slow news periods and did a good turn for the media with stunts that were tiring and without much effort.

A review of some: a lame attempt to trademark "You're fired," a vile attack on another PR-hound, Rosie O'Donnell, before Premiere Week, and a host of strange tirades against Martha Stewart for her failed version of *The Apprentice*, which Trump said brought down his own ratings . . . even though his show was simultaneously boring us to tears.

What attracted viewers in the first place? His smirk is not charming, and regardless of what his wives have stated in the press, there is no lure. In the 2000s, NBC went down the proverbial tubes by pushing a duo-roster of *The Apprentice* and the equally gross *Fear Factor* and forced smart people further from the tube.

Many of us who work in media see this as the point when broadcast television became something you did when there was nothing else to do, as opposed to the previous appointment television viewing. (See the "Appointments Needed" sidebar in "Heads in Air: The New Toy Won't Replace Our First Love.")

Now as DJ Trump fades into hopeful obscurity, he is shlockly hocking "Trump Vodka," "The Trump Haberdashery," "Trump Water," "Trump University," and a series of Trump reality shows about beauty contestants and advice that he needs to bestow upon a puzzled public. Prediction: Trump will be the Pia Zadora of this generation. For those too young or too lazy, Zadora was a popular name in the 1980s, a Paris Hilton–like gal who made a lot of movies, won a Golden Globe for Best Actress [playing someone who, ah, seduced her father—Stacy Keach in what was hardly his finest hour], and then disappeared forever. Her husband was insanely rich, and her backer . . . enough with Pia already.

Here are reasons why we will move into the shinier decade with fewer types like this Trump—*Celebrity Apprentice*'s meager 4.5 rating with bigger stars than DT:

1. Most people are not happy to hear someone flipping off, "You're fired!" with glee. What this world needs is more positive role models, and we'll get them, too.

2. Most people would not hire the actors on *The Apprentice*. Can't we hire our own actors from any local eatery?

3. Most people have been told by the major media that Trump is not as rich as he thinks he is and that many of his developments merely lease his name. Advice from a faker is no longer welcomed. Let's say it together: you can't sell hype to a population that invented hype.

4. Most people don't want to be watching someone who is sexist. His use of the term "gals" was bad enough, but the way he rolled his eyes at the females on his show was painful to watch.

5. Most people standing at the water cooler, or clicking on a virtual one, do not want to admit to their friends they are addicted to a show about an ego-inflamed madman, particularly when we work for one already.

6. Most people do not want their kids to be looking up to someone who is so obviously without morals. (I hear Trump's a teetotaler; that information itself is suspect.)

7. Most people do not want to go eat at a restaurant that uses Trump in its ads, or so studies have proven in recent year. For instance, KFC got embroiled in a scam to hire someone from the show for a finger-licking sales job. The guy didn't accept—and KFC had oil (mud) on its face.

Summing up: we are suddenly figuring out that life is not a game show! Sure, you do have to fight for what you want (the show's decent motto), but not necessarily with the spirit of mean as the guiding force. Finally, do you want to learn from a man who, when you add up all his efforts, is a lot of hot air?

Hey, this boy is no strategic thinker. You know, if my surname were his, I'd be hawking a Trump Bridge Set. That would be humorous Donald.

Machiavellian Skin

TREND: We will stop falling for people who think they can put something over on us . . . !

Take a deep breath. It's alarming that there are so many people living among us who tell us how "tremendous" and "fantastic" we are and can't stop complimenting us for existing.

These people are all fakes.

They recommend you left and right—they tell the world that you're the best at what you do, and you cannot for the life of you figure out why.

There was this nutty (albeit colorful) woman who ran a nonprofit company, who was full of love and cheer and was always telling me how amazing our company was, constantly comparing our work with that of others she'd hired and fired, but in fact we'd just met. It frightened me.

Then there was that very young man who worked for us who constantly told me what a fabulous person I was to work for—he hardly knew me—and I'm not *that* wonderful a boss, I just have a talent to amuse.

These two scary monsters (sorry, Bowie) had a lot in common. This is a kind of non-quid pro quo, a lopsided status situation where one person wants you to think she loves you that much so that you'll watch her back, or at least treat her as if she's your BFF (old people, please go to answers.com/bff).

These people take "keep your enemies closer" to an extreme, because they don't really like you. It's a way to be sure you don't turn on them. See Machiavelli in your history books.

How you recognize this syndrome (and it's not kissing up; that's too easy, so rip that out of your head) is easy: when someone tells you how outstanding you are and you're sure he can't possibly know, you're being victimized by someone who is at best nuts and at worst your newest stalker. What I'd do is ask him directly: "Yes, you love me because I'm lovable and all, but what examples do you have?"

That'll shut him up—or at least confuse him sufficiently to stop the obnoxious beaming.

And, oh yeah, in case you are sitting there thinking, "Why is this problematic?" let me go further . . .

Both the creatures referred to here turned on me for slight infractions; one went so far as to burst into tears and threaten me. My comment that set this off: "What the heck are you going on about?" The return was an aghast claim that she thought I'd do anything for her.

Back on this planet, I made a list of people who wrote me e-mails asking me for a favor without saying what precisely was in it for me or even what they might do with, for, or around me—I'm supposed to jump because I'm supposedly such a cool guy.

The number was 100-plus, including that bizarro who worked at RLM and told me every couple of days how much he "wants to excel in the worst way," only to resign that week. What was he doing? Testing a script?

Machiavellian Skin, friends, can be beaten to the punch. Maybe you can't spell it, but you are sure as hell able to combat cretins who smile as they consider what they get in return for loving you.

In my grandmother's jargon: *bubkas!*

THE ONE-WORD CHAPTER

WHAT'S THE MISSION OF EVERY COMPANY?

Moneymaking.

Sex and Snakes and Couch Jumping

How to Be Sure You're Not Selling to People Who Don't Buy during This Era of Attention-to-Noise Surplus Ratio. Otherwise Known as, "What's This? A Laermer Blog Post?"

TREND: The new sales tactic is to *not* use words or tactics that will amuse your customers, period, but never move them to action.

Pretty attention-grabbing chapter title, right? Well, it's all about getting people to think about what they are giving away when they hope to garner attention online. And fail.

Once, the phrase we heard used to refer to hyping incorrectly was "couch jumping," alluding to the probability that the person marketing the product had gone off the deep end. Then came "snakes on a plane," meaning having the new product talked about endlessly online and screwing with corporate expectations.

Hollywood is elitist in afterthought, considering only what might have worked before, as opposed to what could work in the future. That can be awfully misleading. Hollywood elitism is, incidentally, a Fnord for what I'm really saying. Just don't forget most uppity people are hiding the "fear of fraud" inside them.

I write this at the end of the second weekend of the "hissy little horror flick" *Snakes* (AP's assessment), one week past a Sunday night when so-o many bored arts writers wrote endlessly on how disappointing the $15 million that this typical *Poseidon Adventure/Towering Inferno* story garnered during its first time at bat was.

The writers who went on about *Snakes*'s failure had very little to peg it to, because even though the movie was on everyone's tongue, it didn't actually get any butts in seats. I guess if it had done better, the stories would have been shorter. It's "nothing to say" syndrome when people aren't battening down the hatches because of bad news.

Now, on this very day, everyone in media circles was hoping that the second weekend would be another big news item and finally prove that the Web had "opened" a movie. But blog followers know that movies had been promoted and held up as must-sees on the Web for many years before *Snakes* (successful openings). After all, who was the main audience for Spiderman but those who waxed on about it after seeing McGuire & Company at Comic Con earlier that year?

The people who talked about the Samuel Jackson-and-boa flick were expert Web folks who knew (rather than went to see it) that this movie was not the point.

Even more, the folks who *go* to movies to get out of the house are no longer the same people who are "in the know" about one fact: a movie like *Snakes* will be on cable and in DVD or Time Warner Pay Per View in a matter of seconds nowadays, so why bother with the movie?

It's much more fun to talk about it online while we wait for the inevitable home release.

The fact that so many insta-pundits crassly explained how "this is the first movie changed by the fans" (online eager beavers allegedly made the director pump up the now-known motherfucker line in the movie) points out three basic problems with hype in the modern era, and a few of these should be discussed mightily by anyone who sells for a living.

1. Those putting up sites dedicated to this movie were showing off their ability to make a funny movie idea even funnier. These weren't fans. They were people who felt, rightfully, that their point of view was better and artier than a silly movie about snakes on a plane.

2. The minute Jon Stewart and the Morning Show (my new favorite band) started to pontificate on how this was surely "the summer's biggest movie," "strangely enough," those Web types who made it the talk of the town decided not to watch it in the theaters after all. I mean, Keith Olbermann did so many pieces on this that it stopped being at all mysterious.

3. Those who go to the cinema regularly see movies that look good in previews. They may read about something or watch entertainment stories on TV and then feel like they saw the best parts. Previews. Friends, you need to leave a little mystery; don't give away the cow, right? Gosh, how many TV shows had aired the readily available watered-down clip of Sammy Jack saying that line by the time the movie came out? Plus, the snakes weren't Kermit-adorable, so we didn't want to root for them. Rooting for the humans? We go to *Die Hard* retreads for that.

4. In many interviews I stumbled upon, Jackson, actress Julianna Margulies, and the director David R. Ellis (who dat?) were all heard to say how they didn't want the people at home to "tell them what great art is." Great art?! Also, who's zooming whom? Movies are supposed to be a communal effort. Such talking back to the audience got a lot of people saying to each other on the Web, "Okay, we won't." And they stayed home.

5. Are we the people who sit in seats supposed to be figuring out what you are doing and thank you for doing it? No. Self-effacement works wonders when you're selling something people can live without. In our new, more open world, let's stop telling people what to like!

6. In this case, it was New Line Cinema's fault more than anything. Because the content itself (it turns out this movie had a plot) was never shown online at all. That's a boat that was missed, surely. Instead, the same scenes of Jackson screaming at the constrictors were booed at after a while. The funny bits I witnessed on HBO would have made the attractors go, "That's hilarious. This I got to pay for." Alas, not so much.

7. At one point, Ellis bitched to *Entertainment Weekly*—whose unintentionally hilarious "Will *Snakes* Change Movies Forever?" cover made me pee my pants—that he was afraid that people were thinking his masterpiece was pure camp. "I don't like that," he murmured. It reminded me of *Carrie: The Musical*, the biggest bomb in Broadway history; when I interviewed the director, Terry Mann, he said with a straight face, "This is a Jacobean tragedy" rather than the send-up that it turned out to be.

8. Camp is good. Ask the creators of *The Rocky Horror Picture Show* and *Rambo* if camp, no matter what the maker was

trying to do, doesn't sell tickets. And more times than once. Because camp will out.

To state to the media with no uncertainty that you hope a silly C-level horror filth becomes a renowned noir is artistic ridiculousness *(ridiculousness as art?)*. It also amounts to worthless, mystery-free chatter about something that no one will remember when we meet next year to review summer classics that need to be reenvisioned. That is the biggest shame of all.

9. Ssss!

CC, No No!

TREND: The way of the future will be no CCing. Whatsoever.

C C. That pretty little designation at the top of your e-mails today means more than just Carbon Copy. It should feel synonymous with Corporate Coverage, as of your ass.

You know you've crossed into Corporate Coverage when

1. You receive an e-mail from a coworker asking for details on a project or account.

2. You respond CCing your boss, your coworker's superior, your assistant (if you're lucky), and Legal.

I heard Carl Corporate, another CC whom we know but don't necessarily *always* love, talking about how important it is to play the game of CCing: Carl inundates the higher-ups with so many e-mails, each detailing how he has accomplished a task that is part of his job description, that eventually the H-Us delete the e-mails without looking at them.

It's the greatest (nay, oldest) game played in corporations, and it underlies the largest problem we have as a work culture, one that will disappear as e-mail becomes less "the thing." As e-mail-on-a-diet America becomes reality, we must stop spending time and resources to ensure that we are apparently working, cultivating an atmosphere in which overt kissing tactics are not only smiled upon but promoted as good job, Beanie.

Essentially, when we pretend to work, no work gets completed because e-mails go unanswered. And during the day it's a round robin of folks writing one another nonstop.

Please sigh.

We must stop covering our butts by CCing everyone and anyone. What's better for the future is learning how to just fucking speak up.

So here's what will happen when e-mailing becomes the dodo bird: we will begin to get work done, we will find sight of the importance of what we do, we will take responsibility for what we've done (or haven't done yet), and we will talk loudly in a gracious, respectable manner when it is sincerely time to take credit for something. Yes, Virginia, credit is good.

Everyone will go back to working for a single goal: the mission of a company. (See the chapter "What's the Mission of Every Company?" a few pages back.) If one fails, we all fail, and there's no longer such a thing as taking the fall. No one has to take a single bullet for any team.

Since e-mail is, however, still killing us, there are some tasks to perfect. First, outlaw CCing at your firm (thank me later). "Don't send anyone an e-mail they don't need to respond to" is the rule. Use a meeting where everyone stands up and gets swiftly updated—or updates.

Then you should write a couple of notes to people you work with, the kind you need penmanship for. You'll get responses you never anticipated: appreciation for the time you took.

It appears, says the Emily Post Institute, that just 49 percent of people who want something from someone do it via writing. But 52 percent of respondents in a survey said that they prefer a handwritten note over e-mail—prefer it enough to read it. What's that say?

Imagine writing something that someone actually reads and then responds to. My heart!

But as a South Carolina woman did in 2007, do not write a judge "Kiss my ass" on any judicial paperwork that he or she will see. It's not worth the jail time.

For more on writing letters and CCing fewer people, see Laermer.com/getaclue.

WHAT HAPPENS ON TV STAYS ON TV

BUILDING A
BRAND FROM
PERSONAL
EXPERIENCE

TREND: This is my story. If you want to build a brand, so I discovered without anyone's assist, you'd better use what you've got. In the next decade, pay careful attention to your timing! Your brand's lifespan will be finite, so be careful of limited shelf life.

Allow me a personal rant to make one point. In June of 2004, I got a lot of heat in the town of L.A. when I was chosen to be a host on a new and banally titled reality show on The Learning Channel (TLC) called *Taking Care of Business*. I decided to take it as far as I could, and I got a lesson in how to make something well known even when no one is shitting in the woods, so to speak.

Our show was basic: we went into businesses (a suit store, a skateboard emporium, a limo service, an Internet café, a diner, a sports store, and a baby gift shop) to get them up to speed in a world they seemed unready for.

For me, I dubbed this the era during which I'd do what the Ryan Seacrests of the world make happen all the time: build a platform for the Laermer brand.

Our series (premiering at 10 p.m. after *Trading Spaces*, shuffling off the ungodly not-prime-time hour of 4 p.m.) was all about four "experts" going to failing businesses and making them work. The stores and services we strode into needed some high-level help; in some cases, the landlord was seeking the best way to shut them down. My job was to create high levels of exposure for both the store and all of you at home. And as everyone knows about reality television by now, every scene was staged.

But alas, since I was the "buzz builder" for the program, I had all the right in the world to get a lot of buzz for me. It felt natural.

Here is where the trouble started, and it was a lesson for me—and now, perhaps, for you. Since I had *Full Frontal* PR out, the one about the art as opposed to the science of publicity, I begged, cajoled, and threatened my then-publisher to do a snazzy new version of this piece, tied to the show. Now I had product.

The negotiation to use the *TCOB* logo took about a month— that was a week longer than the publishing of my new edition. Go figure. Lawyers get paid by the hour, publishers by the decade.

Now I had to ratchet up interest in me. The easiest way to get coverage was to ensure that my name and my book were associated with the coverage I could get in the media, particularly since TLC (part of Discovery Communications) was imploding while our show was being prepped. Ah, yes, they fired the general manager and tons of other people as we rolled out. Figuring that I had a mantel from which to shout, I stayed on and sent the show's own two-minute vignette to anyone who might accept the darn thing in pre-YouTube America.

I also figured that since this was a New York show, I'd better hit those people hard. I'd wanted to stand out in Times Square giving out dollar bills *and a nice hint to watch the show* to passersby, but the same well-paid Discovery Comm. legal types said it would be like paying people to watch our show. When A&E did this a few months later, you read about it everywhere. Go figure, part two.

I had to do something mightier in public, since I'd already been on tour at bookstores and marketing associations via my mouth and the incessant e-mailings I like to do. So while some media attention was being bestowed on our "business makeover show," I got my new book out there and got myself some new representation, as people were suddenly eager to help a guy who had already got himself on TV.

I had beaten Famous Lizzie Grubman to the punch as the first PR guy on prime time! Armed with that, I did the first ever "Media Guru First of His Kind on Prime Time" press release— wide—and in doing so I shot-put reminded TV viewers about, for once, an *anti-Apprentice* program with humor and chutzpah and no retold lessons.

Then I did a radio tour, which was kind of a waste of time because during fall 2004 all anyone wanted to talk about was how the then-presidential candidates might treat business in their administrations.

Ah, yes, it was time for a slogan. I went with the Four Bizketeers. It fell flat. I called the national press and got the four of us in *TV Guide*, *Newsweek*, the *New York Times Magazine*, and a few others, all of them with pronounced tie-ins to a certain new book . . .

Then we debuted for real—October 16, 2004. I commenced a full frontal campaign to educators for consideration of my tome as the textbook of choice. I reasoned with anyone who would listen: why should a book on PR *have to* read like an appliance manual?

Aha, a sea change—and by a TV host, no less. I called higher education professors on both coasts and explained why the book is class, all class! And, yes, they assigned it, so I went and did a series of lectures at the first 20.

One-time-only offer! Get your television star! (And, one vanity add-on: I did get my eyelashes dyed to make them flashier for TV. The producer made me.)

Then I got the rights for the audio book back from the publisher and featured it as a how-to class online, free of charge.

Then I created a syndicated radio outing on using the tools of the media to enlarge your exposure.

TCOB ran 13 of our series and then stopped. I always wanted to know how this happens. You don't actually receive a call when you're canceled; the networks merely fade your show to painful black. Of course, none of us wanted to work with TLC again after it asked us to fill out an FBI-like background check, peering into our lives from now back through childhood. We felt that was an invasion of everything, and we didn't want them to know our dirty secrets. I have some. They're doozies.

So finally, I wasn't the new guy on the Amex ads, even though RIM, which makes BlackBerry, started to use me in many media columns as the ultimate speedy communicator!

The bottom line: I discovered that anytime people want you, use it. Everything in a media-saturated world can be a platform for something. One needs to be aggressively creative and think about the next step on the road to whatever.

The best thing that happened to me was that businesses took our advice and an article in a major business magazine summed up what we did in its "Smarts" section—without my having pitched it. Mostly, what I loved was the not-so-subtle headline: "Real-World Business Advice from a Hit Makeover TV Show." Ahem.

First PR and then sales are derived from exposure by television, duh. If you have a platform where people can see you, grab it, don't stop for anything, and see where it goes.

But there's a price to be paid for being out there so much. I was shocked by how many "old pals" contacted me after half-watching the show, which did get terrific reviews even though the network couldn't or wouldn't support it. It was nice to catch up with grade-school friends, I guess, but in the end . . . you guessed it. I was suspicious.

Healthy suspicion came out of the experience because the folks who came out of the woodwork started to offer me everything: a lot of cruddy speaking engagements, offers to consult, a funny bunch who paid all four of us to "do a live demo" of our TV show. (That we did—money.)

I took everything in, listened in a measured way, smiled, and asked about dotted lines. It is the cliché that every businessperson can't help but remember. Often if you build it, they will pay you, thinking "I don't want to miss this boat." Just get it in writing.

Make it Simple, Make It So

Have you ever noticed that nearly every product needs to have a unique branding message or something with unnecessary added value so that you know it's special and the one that you must possess no matter what?

It is not enough to be good; it's important for us to get the idea that this is "the only one" or "nothing else lasts long" or some other stupid slogan. Yet that just confuses people.

Thanks to those Web companies that have succeeded greatly—Google being the champ—the near future will bring us fewer complicated second names and branding messages and more direct . . . directness.

Also, you will see the end of sharing of slogans or logos on machines or Web sites or ads or stores or T-shirts or even microprint (the tiny words you find when you buy anything these days). I'm staring at a Dell right now, and it has several non-Dell logos on it, even on the sides where the disk drives are. It's a little annoying.

I have seen more companies start as, say, "Integrated Fitness Company" (a real example), only to sell the coolly named Fitlinxx product. Guess what the corporation ended up being called so as not to confuse its customers? Then there's Dell, which is a company that keeps naming its brands and internal products until I am confused as to what I'm buying. Can't they all be the Dell 1, 2, and 3 series, like BMW does?

Even Research in Motion should have known better when it came up with the perfect product (BlackBerry, almost from the start), but still insisted on calling the corporation RIM, and I won't go there. . . . I can promise you that BlackBerry will be its corporate name once/if Microsoft overtakes it with its PDA, now that they own Sidekick's parent, Danger Inc.

Or Web sites, which are the worst. People always want to name their site something gorgeous and confusing—*Newsweek* was for years www.msnbc.newsweek.com, in a weird confabulation that was solved in 2007 with the better-late-than-never launch of newsweek.com, while in the same industry, *New York* magazine went with www.newyorkmetro.com for some reason, and *Crain's NY* magazine was all over www.newyork business.com. Guess what both are called now? (www.newyorkmag.com and www.crainsnewyork.com.) It took a bit of time for them to wise up. And I'm certain that the latter will shortly be shortened to www.crainsny.com. Why did CNBC become MSNBC in the early 2000s, only to reappear as CNBC last year? Do people get hired as Corporate Screwing Things Up Officer?

Let's even be a serious for a short paragraph: St. Petersburg, Russia, became Leningrad when the Russian government in 1924 thought it sounded "too German," and after all that expensive rebranding, what's it called today?

An-n-yway, if you are like me, you note with bobble-headed headshaking how silly slogans for products are—and how many of them are tossed in as if a product *had* to have one. I try to buy from companies that believe in their products. I was happy to see A-1 Steak Sauce say, "Yeah. It's That Good," a few years ago. Now I see Staples and Philadelphia Cream Cheese and half a dozen others say the same. Then there are the nine major brands saying, "Think about it." (So, I did.) And I concluded: no one believes in originality. I've stopped buying out of frusration.

Note that Google has zero slogans, and that everything it sells is pure Googleness. Its message is "democratize the Web"—and it says it in a subtle way. The single time Google did not appear in a product name (Froogle, for comparison product searches) ended abruptly, as it is now called Google Product Search.

As a marketing master said: love your brand—whether it be city, Web site, or even German-sounding last name (Laermer.com). Do it any differently and you'll find yourself running back to the original anyway. It just takes a bit longer. Wasting time is not very 10's of you—for damn sure.

Did you catch that joke above on me not wanting to be *self-referential*?

part four

TECHNO-CENTRIC

WHAT'S DAT, EXACTLY?

ANOTHER FABULOUS ANALOGY ABOUT UNNECESSARY TECHNOLOGY

TREND: Nothing that changes the game too much (stops companies from making lots of money in that fastest possible way) will come around to modify the way we get tunes.

When ascertaining the latest trends—a technique that some call "peeling back the onion"—please be caring and derive insight. By looking at some of the Next BTs of yesteryear (and see the "Doodads That Affected Me" sidebar in

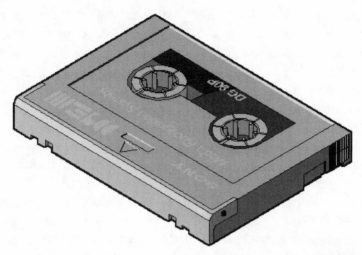

From *Computer Desktop Encyclopedia* © 1998 The Computer Language Co. Inc.

"Sport Mail"), we can better discern the underlying forces at play that influence the trends of not only the present, but the future. A case in point is the quick rise and slow decline of the DAT.

Now, for those who first saw a hospital light after 1990, you may be scratching your head and wondering where the missing "a" at the end of DAT is. This is the acronym for digital audio tape, which was an aha! moment for the Sony Corporation in the mid-1980s. DATs were the much-lauded replacement for ye olde cassette (ask your Dad) tapes of yesterday.

In the 1980s, Sony landed on the best-selling edge of music storage with this product, which provided the same sound quality as a beloved compact disk. Later a computer-grade DAT was introduced (DDS, or digital data storage) so that computers could utilize the large data storage capacity of the medium. At the lowest-quality encoding rate, DAT allowed users to store a whopping (brace yourself) 36 GB!

Mirroring the music piracy wars we listen to now, crazed music industry types went on the offensive to regulate use of the new storage medium, fearing, as they do with P2P file sharing, that DATs' ability to make perfect digital copies of copy-righted music would "cripple" the industry. Recording bigwigs even went so far as to lobby the government to pass the Audio Home Recording Act of 1992 (a.k.a. DAT tax).

Whether it was the recording industry's meddling or simply that consumers thought the teeny tapes were bullshit, the tape format failed to gain the quick popularity needed to make any-one care, outside the insular world of professional and semi-professional music artists (ironic in light of the incessant recording industry objections).

The kind of cheap-cheap storage space available in recent years—200-GB drives for $200 or less—rendered the format more than a little obsolete. This led Sony to announce in 2005(!) that it was discontinuing production of its last line of DATers.

The thing that stands between DAT and an endless night of anachronism is the fact that some of these recorders support SMPTE time-code synchronization for film and TV recording. Even there, DATs are being replaced by modern hard disk recording solutions.

As CDs lose ground to iPods and the better MP3 players that people care to buy, and then as online music purchasing gains more momentum, let's bow our heads to any next great thing that doesn't ask for any sort of longevity. It does appear to the observer (or me) that history is always on the verge of repeat-ing itself: just about anything that asks for a "platform" redo is eventually trampled by the march of progress.

So, the learning here: today's recording medium is tomor-row's museum piece.

Bacn and the Art of Communicating Later

TREND: It's bad enough that we have to answer e-mail; now we need to look at material that we are asked to respond to after we answer all that crap. This is madness.

Now we need to respond to other people's whims no matter how idiotic it is.

"Just because it's a real phenomenon that nobody's bothered to name yet doesn't mean we'll think you're clever for giving it a name," said a friend of mine the other day.

How right, especially if the name for it is stupid. Bacn is an inedible new Internet term that bodes poorly for the future of the Web as a soon-to-be-useless one-to-one communication medium.

Bacn is the things you get that you kind of sort of maybe want.

Bacn is not spam; rather, it refers to messages—e-mail newsletters, so-called friend requests, something you got to fill out on a slow-moving social net server, even checkups on Amazon orders or updates that you "got to do" and the like—that are wanted but not needed. Notifications you might want. But not right now, because you're busy responding to people who actually took the time to ask you a question.

Say you receive e-mail that Some Geek is now following you on Twitter and Jennifer Goldchild just wrote on your Facebook fun wall; that's bacn. Did you need to know it's pronounced "bacon"? It's any e-mail you receive that isn't spam, but isn't exactly a personal message either. Your electronic phone bill is bacn. Your Google Alerts, the ones you have to click on later, are bacn.

This disease has already spread to Germany.

Says one wag: "Sure, you have heard of spam, but have you heard of bacn? Not what you eat for breakfast, but what you find in your e-mail inbox that is legitimate e-mail, but not really worth viewing."

BACN also seems to be an acronym for a new system developed by the Air Force last year, along with a system called TBONE (vegetarians need apply):

> BACN *provides voice relay and bridging between tactical and cellular voice systems. It translates disparate data links that today do not communicate. It also acts as an airborne server that permits data storage and sharing for disadvantaged users, while providing increased situational awareness by correlating tactical and strategic air pictures.*

Everyone wants in on this new gosh-darn fad. After the hullabaloo over bacn, in truth, it appears that nobody wants to open messages that make you work, but often when you're playing with your handheld—still legal in public, whew—you find yourself doing it anyway.

After bacn, I can imagine what's next: Seesage? The mail you get that clogs the Web's already-abused pipes and makes you wonder aloud whether or not it's worth even bothering to turn on the computer since it doesn't return the favor (paraphrase/nod to Kate Walsh). Like ever.

AH, MY IDENTITY

TAKE IT
AT YOUR
OWN RISK

TREND: You might want to be someone else online, but, gee, be careful.

In the Isaac Asimov novel *The Naked Sun*, humans on a sparsely populated planet interact only through holographic representations, being wary of physical contact. They prefer "viewing" to seeing. It's doubtful that 2011 will find us quite so unwilling to meet for business lunches or the neighborhood bowling league (although, with luck, we will have the Solarians' robot servants).

But the astonishing growth of social networking sites and virtual communities during the latest digital boom provides, could be for the first time, an actual laboratory for the thought experiments that Asimov, William Gibson, and their peers devised long ago. What happens when community leaves geography behind? Where do we end and our digital selves begin? What is online identity?

Online identity is one thing above all else: malleable.

> Technology allows anyone to augment, mold, shape, shift, accentuate, obscure, and otherwise render herself however she sees fit.

The holographs that Asimov and George Lucas concocted are, in a peculiar way, obsolete without ever having been achieved. Because the guiding aesthetic in online "living" is not Realism . . . it's Impressionism. We have unprecedented control over who we are online, which, increasingly, is *actually* who we are.

The lines have certainly blurred. A *Wall Street Journal* story that flew around the Internet recounted how a man who spent most of his waking hours attending to his virtual self (represented as an avatar) on the Second Life game/software eventually pushed his real-life wife too far by, um, marrying his avatar to another woman. Some observers would say that his actions are tantamount to adultery. Others might question why someone would begin a fantasy life in a gorgeously artificial universe of his own design . . . only to work, settle down, walk the dog, pay a mortgage.

The underlying point: if your real-life body is tethered to a monitor for 12 hours at a time so as to foster a richly textured virtual life, perhaps there is no longer a meaningful distinction. So why sacrifice one for the other, real for fake? Online, the man told the reporter, "You're in total control." His avatar—an ageless, younger, stronger, more successful version of himself—was not just who he wanted to be. It was, with each additional minute he invested, who he *could* be.

As our new favorite decade gets closer, the contours of the online landscape and its intersection with "identity" continue to be defined. Sony sued a player of its EverQuest program who sought to sell his online persona on eBay. Sony argued that the sale was of a "character," and therefore its intellectual property. The player, though, believed it to be his own creation. Like an author who uses Microsoft Word to write a novel. What constitutes virtual identity: the pixels (Sony's) or the personality (the user's)?

Of course, avatars—or virtual reality, or holographs, or whatever digital "bodies" we inhabit in the next several years—alone do not explain "online identity." One needn't register for Second Life to have a "second life" online. The details, secrets, and nuances of our banal experiences back in the brick-and-mortar world (the one with actual mortgages and dog walks that require a baggy) are migrating to the Internet in ever-greater numbers every day. Blogging, MySpacing, Facebooking, Googling, Beboing, YouTubing, and dozens of other habits have mined bottomless reserves of narcissism and voyeurism to make our online "selves"—the personas broadcast to the masses—more prominent than ever. If identity is equal parts fact and perception, its transition to a global digital community means that it is as fluid as its owner chooses.

Perhaps 10 or 15 years ago, the most common question pertaining to online identity might have been: "What does my e-mail address say about me?" CuteGirl22@aol.com was the lone personal signage for the average new arrival on the information superhighway. Such quaint personal distinctions disappeared with the dial-up modem. The sheer tonnage of information created by, created about, and available to each of us means that, by default, our online identities are here for the long haul.

Individuals still retain most of the control. The nature of our personality/identity is changed less than its reach. Reputations can be made and ruined, and fame or infamy gained, much more quickly, and far more expansively, than even a year ago.

As we shop, love, invest, fight, and participate online, as our interaction grows richer and more involved, the keyboard will begin to say more about who we are than the mirror. Within its limits, the Internet has made each of us his or her own Creator. As those limits broaden, so too does the power of online identity.

Asimov's future envisioned the mixture of freedom and imprisonment that a society encountered when technology allowed each of its members to retreat to a corner. Ours will mix freedom and imprisonment as those boundaries dissolve and we are brought, flat screen by flat screen, into the same solitary and digital room.

Give Me Some Couch Love, Babe, Yeah, Give It to Me, Oh, Oh

TREND: We don't need money to travel—just get there and plop on a stranger's sofa. Interactivity now at its finest.

A new phenomenon is taking the couch's sullied reputation as that age-old bastion of inertia and, like the quarters within, flipping it inside out. Couch surfing—yes, you read that right—has surfaced, and it's a movement that lends a seriously new cachet to old sofas.

Originated by inveterate globetrotter emeritus Casey Fenton—who blindly e-mailed 1,500 Icelandic students for travel tips before visiting their country, only to receive a surprising number of offers to "house" him—CouchSurfing (yes, I know: a smushed-together brand) claims to have 280,000 participants in 218 countries, including more than 70,000 in the United

States. In a few short years it has grown from a handful of friends looking to travel cheaply into an organic social network whose members see their mission as nothing less than an effort to create a better world, one couch at a time.

And as a man who loves couches—ask any I've fallen for—this makes it a good world.

So, truly, Fenton and his fellow surfers have married the social networking power of the digital age to the brick-and-mortar hospitality of previous generations, and the resulting system has flourished among people across nearly every demographic line.

Hosts volunteer accommodations—be it an actual couch, a spare bed, or something else—for surfers, who reciprocate with hospitality in their own home cities and countries. The arrangement allows travelers to journey widely and inexpensively, while also facilitating meaningful connections among people and places.

The Revolution we are undergoing (hope, hope) takes seriously the task of easing travel, education, cultural immersion and exchange, and the building of friendships—perhaps as far as one can get from egregious couch potato-ry.

If the Net knocks down barriers by distributing information freely and easing communication and friendship—Skype, Instant Messaging, gaming, and so on—then CouchSurfing takes this to the next level by distributing people. Built upon trust in strangers and ending in face-to-face interaction, the surfing community represents cultural exchange on a vast scale, but with a nature that belies several assumptions about online.

Vive the real world, and get off the couch for a reason, y'all.

It's unlikely that the surfboard industry will find as much to protest as Britain's potato farmers (see the chapter "One

Potato, Two Potatoes Later"). Whereas the archetypal couch potato is a socially averse, passive homebody who is curious only about what images will flash across his screen next, the couch surfer is an engaged and active man or woman of the world whose futon is not a fortress, but a meeting post.

> The couch surfer is an engaged and active man or woman of the world.

BATTERY MANAGEMENT CORP.

ONE FURTHER STEP IN OUR QUEST FOR POWER

TREND: Debbie Boone gets a cheap thrill. A coming battery is so thin and waferlike that you can *easily* light up your life.

Every device known to man has to have its own freaking power source. At this point, it does appear that the battery companies own us. Where would we be without lithium ion, I wonder? And are fat batteries better than thin ones? It's enough to make me take a night course.

However . . . there are so many devices out there now that I wonder if we'll all be having part-time jobs keeping them with us and charged. In preparing for this chapter, I actually researched the myriad of spare charging devices and power sources available. The list was so long, I decided to scrap it. Do you think I can spend all year annotating?

Let me cut to the chase—promise.

By the new decade's dawn, a battery like none other will be part of our supercharged life—a paper battery, designed by researchers at Rensselaer University in Troy, New York.

See, a battery uses electrodes, electrolytes, and a separator to chemically store energy. This new battery constructs the three components so that it can be bent, rolled, twisted, and cut to size like a piece of paper. It is in reality a piece of paper.

The separator in this battery is not made of plastic, but rather of wood cellulose, or a kind of paper! Since the actual electrolyte is liquid-based, this battery can work in extreme cold or heat. Normally lead electrodes of the battery type (due to appear in hardware stores in 2011) use carbon nanotubes to make sparks. This cylinder is really small, so much so you can't see it or make contact with it. The battery is less toxic than the ones that burn your fingers, so you are going to see it used in tools—and in medicine! According to the Rensselaer scientists, human blood, sweat, and urine can activate this battery if you set it so that they will (e.g., your human contact with the battery starts it up). So it's something that can release energy slowly over time or all at once, as with devices used to start a motor.

To increase the voltage of electricity, the paper battery would be printed back to back like a ream of paper. To up the power, sheets would be stacked on top of one another.

In 1993, this excited battery fanatic did the PR for a firm that launched the flat flashcard for Lumatec Industries of Austin. That piece, now a relic, was the first use of a flat battery in anything other than simple Polaroid cameras. It was astonishing how tiny this battery was. And that was such a long time ago, before digits were our lives.

Now the notion of flashlights that you could use from inside your nails is not too far away.

The Day the Battery Died

I was sitting on a commuter train when suddenly I realized that my BlackBerry had gone kaput.

It was a bizarre feeling to be on a train without someone to talk to. Sure, I'd done it before, but when?

What to do . . . what to do. The tiny hairs on the back of my neck stood up. It was so unusual. And no, I had no phone with me. I suppose I could have talked to the person sitting next to me, but he was busy tapping away. An interruption looked unwelcome—and fiercely so.

What about reading? I had nothing. Where's *Amtrak* magazine when you need it? Inside my pocket were nothing but receipts that were crinkled to the point of being unreadable and a note to myself that I decided it was best to ignore.

Thinking. I hadn't done that in a while.

Wondered if there was a spare battery in my knapsack (and no, my newspaper was read already and, like the Grisham novel, had been tossed earlier today). Riffled through. Found a snack. An old one. Yuck. A really old one. No spares. Where's a spare when you need it? Right. It's charging at home. Useless charging pad. Now, what about that thinking thing!

I started to think about the number of people who respond to phone, e-mail, and in-person statements with "Sounds good" or its inbred cousin "Sounds great." And then I made a list. This was kind of fun because that turns out to be a mirror of those I'm going to send a card to that says Sounds Good on it 50 times, like Bart's opening credit bulletin board.

Okay, so now my pen's dying. This is turning out to be a day of ironies after all. Back to thinking—this time nothing in writing, Richard. Who is the person I most want to be when I grow up? Let's see. This is a good game to play, not too taxing and not too boring. I want to be Alan Alda. No, no actors. Why Alan Alda, though? I guess because he seems to get better at his craft with age. Still, no actors.

I can't think of anyone I admire today. So I'm going to look out the window at Croton. People look a little sad today. Must be the weather. Is the sky really gray? How do days get gray? I think it's more of a dullish blue. I wonder where the perfect weather is. Some say San Diego, others Belize.

I need my BlackBerry. It's life, it's death, it's purgatory when it's out of my hands. Oh, why did that battery have to die? If sitting and staring ever comes back into fashion, give me a shout. But remember, yell loudly.

COMPUTER
IS GONE—
IS LIFE?

TREND: When your computer shuts down and you can't get it back on, it'll make you sick.

For months, and maybe years, before the Y2K New Year's celebration, companies and citizens alike were tensed and readying themselves. As the ball dropped, a collective breath was held, and then . . . nothing happened. There were no explosions, no power outages that engulfed the entire northern hemisphere; the utilities didn't shut off, and the human race was not annihilated because of faulty coding attached to nuclear weapons. The best that anyone got was Grandma snoring on the couch and a few corporate execs pissed because they had spent countless hours and reams of cash hoping to "fix" the Y2K bug that had everyone terrified.

Maybe Grandma had it right. The relevance of Y2K—or rather, the fear that accompanied its arrival (and then passing)—had more to do with a superconscious dependence on the computers that we allow to run our lives and maintain our survival. Those who were less reliant on computers for their daily existence could sleep easily . . . but who, in today's world, could snore soundly through another such episode?

The potential for crisis is always there, perhaps at the boundaries of our vision, whether it be a computer crash that angers patrons at a DMV in New Jersey (and if there is one state where you do not want angry drivers . . .) or a glitch on a system at your local hospital where you depend on the computer system to get patients' health history—not to mention run the machines that keep them alive on a minute-to-minute basis.

Fine, computers are important—you win—Uncle! And perhaps you're not worried about the DMV (you live in New York, where drivers are rational) and you're not planning on checking into the hospital any time soon—but the very idea of trying to log onto MySpace to check out what Ted has replied to your "Your date is a skank" comment, only to be turned away by a downed server? Now you know what real terror is.

We've all been there, whether it's continually hitting the "refresh" button on our LiveJournal page or screaming at our screen when Vimeo takes too long to load. Seriously, don't they know that you have a social life to take part in? What would happen if you had to go to bed tonight without checking in with your 1,393 friends (and Tom)?

The thought of our beloved Internet and computers not being there for us in the future is horrifying, true, but the thought of living for even a moment without our social networking sites? That's death to the common man: how many others are having fun out there on the Net, without you, right now? Freelance graphic artist Nathan Lewis describes it as "The feeling is kind of akin to getting dumped by a chick. And then you get jealous thinking about all the people having fun with your ex."

A joint Yahoo!/OMD (the media agency)-sponsored study innocuously entitled "Internet Deprivation Study" reminded us how dependent we are on being online to get our daily intake of socializing: nearly half of the respondents couldn't go without the Net for more than two weeks, and the median time the subjects could go without being online was five days. This paragraph and the next two are brought to you by a very long, reasonably unwell-written press release by Yahoo! on September 22, 2004, about OMD and Yahoo! examining consumers' media habits "and their emotional connection towards the Internet (whatever)." Its findings were in line to be discussed that day at the Harvard Club as part of Advertising Week, a yearly venture sponsored by *Ad Age* magazine.

Again and again, respondents without access to the Internet complained of feeling "out of the loop"; irrespective of their demographic background, the subjects of Yahoo!/OMD's study described feeling a sense "of loss, frustration and disconnectedness" when they had absolutely zip-o access.

This not only demonstrates our reliance on computers for the, you know, life-threatening stuff, but once and for all demonstrates the power the Internet has over our social lives. Wenda Harris Millard, then Yahoo! Chief! Sales! Officer!, said: "Deep ethnographic research like this enables us to do much more than look at consumer trends, it allows a rare glimpse into the reasons consumers make the choices they do and how they are emotionally impacted. We can then help marketers apply these insights to reach their target audiences."

We recognize that our target audience goes through withdrawal after a short period of time offline—in a way that they perhaps never felt about watching their television or attending a sports game in a highly sponsored arena. This recognition should serve as a conduit for establishing and maintaining a relationship with our target audience.

At the very least, we should know what makes our audience tick, and if six hours of Friendster will make them tear up like they are chopping onions, perhaps that emotional connection is something marketers should be aware of. If nothing else, a marketer's job is to make buying and using its product/service an emotional venture—what can we learn (and take away) from how people engage one another on the Internet?

What I Said about the 2000s: A Look Back as I Pat Myself on the Back

In the many learned pages of *TrendSpotting* (2002), I had fun musing about the wild inventions coming our way in a series titled "Think Like *The Jetsons*." Here were my thoughts—far-out and often sensational and finally, darn accurate.

Kids, you may look forward to, among other notions, this to occur in your lives . . .

- Robotics grows as big as the PC in your life. It will allow for a constant connection to everything in your home, and it won't even annoy you as much as the Microsoft paperclip "helper."

- The phone bill will suddenly be the billing mechanism for most out-of-home objects—you can buy a Coke with your phone.

- Implants will help us keep track of everyone, at all times.

- Windows in the house will do a lot more than let sunlight in.

- Food and household items will be ordered from kiosks in your home.

- Your doctor will prescribe a microchip implant instead of a pill.

Which came true? How about every single darn one? I also mentioned how actor Jon Tenney was featured in six TV shows in the 1990s and nothing clicked. I beseeched Hollywood to give him a good job, and he's now the fiancé on *The Closer*. Way to go. Here I must shamefully say that I spelled his name wrong in the last book. I'm more responsible—and able to admit fault.

Today there are computers that are programmed to see and hear and react to other sensory stimuli. Nowadays, physical interaction with your computer is less than common. No more entering appointments into your calendar; you do it via a virtual assistant (call it BlackBerry), and information is checked for conflicts and entered in for you. Through all this syncing, it automatically notifies you that you have "something to do." What it is is better management of life's little annoyances like work and other frictions in life.

The phone is about to become a wand, thanks to a new acronym that you will be seeing everywhere. The near field communication system, or NFC, is a short-range wireless technology that enables communication between devices over a short distance (hand's width). The technology is primarily aimed at usage in mobile phones, and it's in test already, working by magnetic field induction and operating on an unlicensed radio-frequency band. You can use it for public transportation in several cities already—buses, baby!

Just like America (and so can you, Colbert!), there is no standard protocol in the world's superpower for tech. In a funny, ironic, and just-deserts digression, the new entertainment format, the high-definition version of DVDs, also supported by no standard, was called a "yawn" (quotes mine) in a recent survey of consumers, who couldn't be bothered deciding.

A patent licensing program for NFC is currently under development by Via Licensing Corp., part of Dolby Laboratories, which means unfortunately that there won't be a standard, and it will be fought over by The New Cingular and an Asian mobile firm that owns the rights to a single "type" of NFC.

A firm with the too-subtle moniker Research Frontiers introduced SPD-Smart Glass Panes that really do eliminate the need, digitally, for blinds and drapes because, face it, the home has to be more easily managed and save you money rather than eat up the cash.

What's amazing is that for 5,000 years, glass has remained pretty much the same. Safety, sure, bulletproof glass I got, but glass was it until now. Much like the liquid crystal display of your digital watch, the product is really "electrochromic" glass. A thin layer of electric circuitry suspended underneath a glass layer enables you to control the characteristics of the window, making it either opaque or completely clear with the turn of a dial or through a sensor that adjusts it to changes in the weather or the number of people in a room. Your window, because it will have circuitry in it, could be turned into a computer monitor or an entertainment center for TVs and iPods. Wizardry, for real.

Food and household items ordered from kiosks—that's happening thanks to everything being connected. In dozens of interviews, perky no-kids, double-income family members (the lowly, über-admired DINKs) said that outside of work, 50 percent of their time was spent hanging in the kitchen area. To answer this, smart companies like Whirlpool have developed kitchen computers that absolutely divide the labor—between you and your device. Your S.O. (significant-o) may not be the one who does the shopping, but he sure will happily do the ordering of groceries on the kitchen appliance with you. It's easier than changing diapers, for sure, and you get to do something . . . totally together.

Instead of taking a pill, such as an antidepressant, to alter your mood, microchip implanting has earnestly begun! Everything that was being done chemically is now electronic. Instead of drinking coffee, we are now sending that sensation to the brain. And in the next few years, a person's movement or sensory manipulation will lay the foundation for sending and receiving, yep, signals from brain to brain. Let's call that mind reading via implant!

Imagine the next decade as we begin to monitor the better-operating workforce in less expensive countries: an implant in an employee transmits knowledge of the person's heart rate, how many breaks the person takes, and what part of the office the person is really in!

"Oh, what a world my parents gave me," according to Rufus Wainright's restless wink. "Life Is Beautiful" (splattered) on the *New York Times.*

HEADS IN AIR

THE NEW TOY WON'T REPLACE OUR FIRST LOVE

TREND: Toys of a new sort will replace the portable digital assistant. But nothing will ever make us feel the giddiness we got from our first mobile phone. Don't be sad.

George Orwell couldn't have envisioned what we have today. Millions of people walking around with their new toys pressed to their ears—nothing too private to share with the stranger who happens to whiff it. Ah, yes, people in meetings doing the "BlackBerry bob" (see "Terms I Made Up + Newfangled Future Speak"): half the time going on about something and the other half seeing who wants them below, right on their lap, ignoring those present while they carry on two conversations. Wait. I'm describing myself!

What I am explaining is a perfect scenario for *conspiracists*, of which I am happy to report I am one. You walk down an avenue and watch the people hard at work, not paying attention to anything; I mean, nothing is as important as what's onscreen. Imagine what it's like for them when the batteries die. Then laugh while you can (evil grin).

If we think about it, and the problem is that we have not, the fact that we're not experiencing what's around us Quick, the government is doing something bad, or is it? How would you know? is only the smallest problem here, and it's why when New Toy Syndrome dies out in the next few years, and the PDA becomes just another seminuisance to keep track of (like pets, children, lovers, and house keys), we will have something to look back on with glee.

"Can you believe what all those people looked like with their phones plastered to their ear?" we will say to one another, as if those people were a different race from the "we" we left out!

And my favorite-to-be: "What were *they* all talking about?"

The mediocrity experienced during the 2000s can be traced to the first day a mobile phone got cheap enough to be given away with boxes of Tide. And it has everything to do with using mobile phones to say anything but anything valuable. If an entire population babbles endlessly on phones or scribbles IMs instead of conversing on topics of importance, then trivia is all that matters. It's just talk. In order to have movement or progress, you have to get beyond talk and into opinion or decision making.

If we never take a stance, ever, then those who are making the rules win every time. That means that one day a collective us will wake up and realize that we missed the point . . . that there is no point. So all those years of "checking in" actually made us check out!

In 2011, or hopefully before, we will put down the phone, rub our tired (good) ear, and say, ruefully, "What the—?" It's like in sci-fi when we realize that the frustrated human chasing the android is a robot after all.

In the end: what were *we* all talking about?

Okay, the preachy part of the essay is finished. Let's get to the fun. Say, what will be the toy that replaces our PDAs? Could it be virtual reality sunglasses? Maybe we'll end up with a sensor in our fingertip that allows us to purchase items at will? Or, hmm, let's look out for a paper-thin book that will hold the next hotly anticipated edition of 2011?

None of the above—and all of the above.

You could forecast a thousand different high-fad trends that will come and go in the next 10 years. Cheap technology is simply a matter of imagination coupled with funding (joined at the hip with slick salesmanship). Because since the 1970s and the advent of the mood ring and the telephone answering machine—a double whammy that none of us moody dialers then will forget or forgive—we have always been about the new gadget affecting us and moving our lives along, and the snake-oil salesperson selling us on the idea that, yep, it makes us feel up-to-date, sophisticated, on the road to somewhere.

And so we will always have a new toy to look forward to.

I guarantee that it will never be something that will make us feel as happy as our first mobile phone did. Nuh-uh.

Appointments Needed

TREND: TV networks and cable companies made "appointment TV" go poof.

Like you—except I admit it freely—I'm a big TV watcher. The problem is, I've got no one to talk to about it because I'm not watching it when it airs, and particularly not on TV.

It's pretty groovy that we can get our TV on our phones, I-devices, and even a refrigerator nowadays, but the problem for the business world is that word of mouth is being lost because people don't all tune in at approximately the same moment.

If I were a broadcaster or a producer or a scheduler or even a secretary who rises and falls on the fortunes of the world of episodic TV, I'd be scared shitless.

Can you imagine 1989? Back then, 30 million people watched *The Simpsons* on a network to which only two-thirds of the country had access, and it was a cartoon? I get that we have all sorts of choices now—but you can bet that on Monday after *The Simpsons* aired, 99 percent of the people at work were standing by the watercooler, drinking Volvic and chatting about Marge's nonconformist outbursts or Bart's blue hair (I realize it's the other way round!).

Today, a mere 8.6 million people zooming in on *Samantha Who?* is considered a miracle on network TV, which considering that a little over 100 percent of us have access to ABC is the definition of paltry.

And it shocks me to think that a success is a show that stays on the air, like Donny Deutsch's *The Big Idea*, whose ratings are around 50,000 (!) eyeball-devotees! A well-oiled rumor is that Donny pays half or more of the costs to keep him in bathed lights. Or even a Showtime "hit" like *The Tudors* touts a series high of 465,000—and gets renewed with faux nervewracking celebration.

I watch *Grey's Anatomy* on my Zune four days after it airs, and a friend of mine catches up with it on DVD six months after we ignore the endless reruns. We never discuss it. I got to say those doctors are such bitches to one another that they make me scream sometimes! It's to myself. I sometimes wonder why I even bother starting any of the new TV shows when the networks (it's usually the fraidy cat NBC) are likely to cancel them and screw me up in the middle of an arc. Why did she kiss him, anyway? And is that really her daughter!

Finally, sometimes I'll tune into a heavy drama on one of the cable networks and forget to set my TiVo, so I'm watching it live. The hemorrhoid commercial that follows a jovial moment between the main twosome is really a jolt and makes me long for even the worst HBO (it's called *Dane Cook's Tour*). These ornery breaks snap the tension in the series movement, and as I scream at the TV—realizing it's inanimate—I think to myself, "Why am I doing this?"

Entertainment should make us scream when it's scary. So good-bye to the tube and hello to the devices, and no, I won't be talking to you about TV any longer.

AND FINALLY, EID (E-MAIL IS DEATH)

LONG LIVE NEW MASS COMMUNICATION

TREND: Here are the reasons we will all turn off our e-mail accounts in the next few years, and here's what will replace it (and it'll be ever so gradual).

All right, people, let's all sing with sanity for once.

Your e-mail is out. I'm not talking about it being on the fritz where you say to yourself, "Take a deep breath, it'll be fine." No. You will soon hate the thought of it! According to the Pew Internet Study of 2005, almost half of Web-using teens ("the future of our world," quotes mine) prefer to use IM instead of e-mailing. Twitter, Facebook, and the like have made it so much more popular than Hotmail could ever be, so let's get used to it posthaste.

How ridiculous was the moment that I, a long-known-about e-mail addict (a *US News & World Report* article, "So That's Why

They Call Them Users," quotes the author, a/k/a me, saying that e-mail is "as integral to my life as my frontal lobes"), realized that the person I e-mailed the most, my second in command at my company, left me a note and I wasn't sure who "me" was? Unrecognizable handwriting is unacceptable—and dastardly weird.

Question: Do you write people, or do you communicate with them? Probably the former. Let's talk about what that means.

Oh, let's.

Every single e-mail you get is junk, even the ones you want—junk. I am shocked at how much people send us that we don't want. Do they think we could possibly like them even less?

In 2007 *Slate* took a stance: "It's not hard to imagine a future communications command center where, on a single screen, you'll be able to choose between sending an e-mail, instant message, status note, or blog post—or sending all of them at once—and then have all those bits of text neatly and securely archived."

I think differently. It's time for devices carrying preapproved messages so that e-mail is not as crucial. These will be here in the next five years, because as soon as the New Toy syndrome of near-instant messages from strangers becomes as annoying as an unheard message on a voice mailbox, handy portable machines will appear that will assign particular people the "right" to send you a note. They won't just do it. You won't let them.

On the second, more complicated hand will be inbox creations so that companies can alert you to news or commentary (or even good deals) that will arrive on your desktop for you to see—when you want to, or if. For instance, CES (the Consumer Electronics Show, which hosts billions of products, hangers-on, publicity seekers, and their competitors in Vegas every January) offered a "communication tool," a CES Alert Icon that would appear in your system tray on a desktop and notify the password-protected recipient of deadlines and important announcements directly from CES. Not to belabor the point, but as with everything else, I had to negotiate access. Even though I was sent an invitation, after installing the mega-app, I got: "CES Alert is unable to identify you. Please right-click on the CES Alert icon at the bottom of your screen (in the system tray) and select Login Setup. Then, enter the requested information." I'd entered it as the freakazoid installed. Hours later, I'm wondering if *anything* works as advertised. It looked like this:

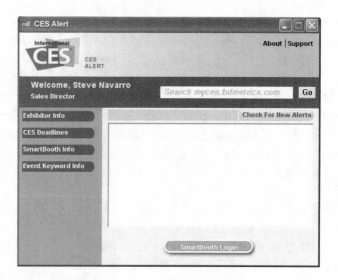

It's all going to happen whether we like it or not. We won't get as much buzz about ourselves, but as any junkie will tell you, eventually the craving to read about "you" will cease. Many of our worst habits have been formed via e-mail. For instance, we have learned to be an insanely passive-aggressive citizenry (me too), and the pre-okayed carrier (name TBD, but I'm thinking The Generator) will be only for friends or those we truly want to talk to . . . so it's going to be a device for good and not evil. So the new little machines will not one be of those "write me and I'll make sure you are not stopped by my

Spaminator" type devices. The tiny little machine will accept only those that we tell it are okay.

Also, it will be encrypted in every way human beings know how, so that no one will be able to usurp it, even at work. Ha! Those bosses like me who want to know everything will finally not be able to kill the cat that wants to know everything.

When only those you enjoy talking to are talking to you, you'll be more caring. Once again you'll begin to use language with verve and some sense of responsibility. You'll treat your native tongue in style—like the bitch it wants to be.

SPORT MAIL

TREND: How to check up on people whom you used to communicate with—and have a good time at their expense until the e-mail well runs dry.

I'm not above reruns, so let me say again: e-mail has become useless. Let's do the math. *Reader's Digest* reports that the average corporate e-mail user sends and receives 133 messages per day. By 2009, when the crescendo starts to take effect and we all wonder why the hell we do it, you'll have at least 160 in your box every day.

So let me offer you a decent use for something you have with you all the time but can't get rid of, like that friend from high school. You've got to learn to play a game with it (or him). Here are the rules:

1. Go to gmail.com or hotmail.com and open an account with a name that is not at all like yours.

2. Make a list of people you hope are no longer at their current position, just to see if you were right about their prospects.

3. Write a letter that says something like this: "Hello, sir/madam. I am wondering if you are still at the job you never deserved in the first place. If you are, please confirm."

4. Send it, unsigned, and wait for some stuff: a. The bounce-back that says, "This address is no longer valid at the domain you wrote to." b. The nasty response that cannot be traced, ha ha ha. c. The curious one. d. Nothing.

5. If it is the first of the bunch, you win by default. If the last, you have opened up Round Two.

6. Send a new note, this time saying, "Come on, dude. I was just messing with you. How are things going?"

7. If you receive a response, you enter the Bonus Round. It is at this point that you can do what the best in the field do, which is make the recipients' heads spin and, as the best way of getting even, just make them think how self-important they truly are.

8. Letters should be sent 10 in a row, then stop for a few days. After that, you can start in again.

9. These e-bombs should always be sent with the intent to make people feel they have someone watching them. This way the people are always on their toes.

10. Enjoy the game. Fairly soon the competition will end. And in the end you will have gotten her/him fired for wasting too much time responding to spam.

Doodads That Affected Me: A Wistful Reminiscence

What are the contraptions that give us a "cannot live without" feeling, as though to think, "How did we ever exist before it appeared on the scene?"

Like, let's talk about Twitter, the unbelievably popular social networking destination where folks can follow me and my every movement— how'd I ever get through a day without being able to shoot a pic of me picking my nose to you? I can't imagine.

In the next decade, we will be searching for something that will make our day-to-day activities that much easier. And before you know it, the stuff from the past will be but a memory. It's important to remember the past as you grab onto the newest gimmick. In the last year, many companies tried with no success to prove that what they sold would be our "to die for" device; examples are endless. Take Pocket Dish by Dish TV. It looked like the perfect idea: a tiny device on which you downloaded programming from your satellite for free. It was a manufacturing nightmare because the device cost over $600, and no one bit; subsequently, say news reports, it was threatened by the major Hollywood studios, who said, "You're kidding. That would mean no more DVD sales!" The device cost the parent company millions. Yet pocketdish.com is still on the site—each size PD is sold out (as if).

What happened to the products of the past? Here is my own list of can't-do-without-it things, in order of importance, and remember the years listed are when I got hooked. Send your additions to Laermer.com/bogglesthemind.

1. *Answering machine* (1979). What? No answering the phone! The problem was, I spent hours creating the perfect outgoing message; the music was never quite right.

2. *Video recorder* (1983). The *M*A*S*H* finale on video was a moment in time. But what about that flashing 12:00—12:00—12:00?

3. *Personal computer by Tandy* (1981), the one with the single floppy drive! I just loved tapping away. I would put in one "operating" disk followed by the one that kept my information—and hope that the coffee cup didn't mistake the thing for a coaster.

4. *Brick* (1990). That phone was larger than my head, but man, pushing the "send" key was liberating. Yeah, the battery lasted a little over 10 minutes.

5. *Whizzer, Etch-a-Sketch, WinkyDink* (don't know what year). These toys kept me alive! Living in a suburban shopping mall, all I had to keep me company were threefold gadgets: a whizzing top, something that magically let me draw without pens (and that stayed where I froze it), and this absolutely splendid transparency that I placed over my black and white TV and drew over it during a show that seemed to portray what I'd drawn. Gosh.

6. *My reel-to-reel* (1975). Laugh all you want. Insert Stewie's poignant snortle from *Family Guy.* But back when there was one phone and one ring type, and when e-mails were "futuristic" communication modes, and most of us wrote longhand, this was powerful machinery—and the music recorded onto a reel sounded better than on any cassette deck you had! My uncoordinated fingers made for smushed tape—an adventure and hard work, and I loved every second of it.

Number 6 was tied with another: 700 numbers that MCI invented in the early 1990s that would follow you wherever you went. You'd put in various numbers—home then office then concubine—and it would really go after you: seven rings with no answer, then next stop. It was a hoot. Imagine not having a phone at your side for every beck and whim and call. And just saying "MCI" after its founder went to prison—that's funny too.

7. *Caller ID* (1995). Staring at a number that came in . . . more liberation. Good: shocking people by knowing it was them. Bad: no more prank phone calls. How, then, could I regress? A lot of people loved the Star 69 phenom, but it always seemed like too much work.

8. *Replay* (1999). Forget TiVo. The device that I treat with kid gloves years later is a digital virtual recorder that automatically skips the commercials as soon as they (very loudly) appear. The networks sued SonicBlue, and so you can't buy one. Make me an offer.

9. *Mini-disc!* (2003). Yes, this was pure form over function: a gorgeous bright blue square machine that took square disklike recordable music. MD was a cult that, like Sony's Betamax, never caught on. I got excited because, unlike CDs, you really couldn't break those tiny diskettes. And for those keeping score, yep, I owned a Newton, too! I admit publicly that I sorely miss Mailgrams, which for all of you going wow-I-remember-those was a results-getting $3 exclamation point in the mail courtesy of Western Union. Those blue envelopes elicited emotion!

10. *Home phone disconnection* (2003). What better moment was there than the technological wonder of *turning off your phone* at home? Let me just say, as someone who moved seven times in nine years, calling Ma Bell and saying, "Cut me off, please," was a thrill that only a true technophile whose mobile phone worked almost everywhere could appreciate.

Hɪ-Tᴇᴄʜ

Tʜᴇ Nᴇᴡ Nᴇᴡ ᴀɴᴅ Iᴍᴘʀᴏᴠᴇᴅ

TREND: We stop being wowed by supertechnological talk; it's a mere marketing term saying, "I'm a breakthrough and a miracle." This book is hi-tech.

Yesterday's "hi-tech" is today's new and improved—namely, the phase of a brand when someone announces that you never knew it, but you can't live without this. It occurs because of the degree of proliferation of everything. But, as my colleagues who toil in technology tell me with a shrug, ubiquity eventually overshadows novelty.

Ubiquity eventually overshadows novelty.

LCD tech is today's example I'll use in class. This was implemented 35 years ago and can now be found on virtually every device or appliance imaginable—but still, because someone always wants to make a living, you will now be hit over the head with OLED!

Sony Corp. recently announced the world's first commercial launch of ultra-thin televisions using organic light-emitting diode (OLED) technology, aiming, said the press release, "to revive its reputation for innovation. The next generation television has a screen with a thickness of just three millimeters (0.12 inches), which was made possible because the organic display is self-luminescent and does not require a backlight."

According to IEEE.org, which is the world's "leading professional association for the advancement of technology," here is *The History of Liquid Crystal Displays*:

> *The modern history of liquid crystals has been dominated by the development of electronic displays. These developments began in 1964, when . . . RCA Laboratories discovered the . . . dynamic scattering mode. . . . In the beginning liquid crystal displays (LCDs) were limited to niche applications such as small-size displays for digital watches, pocket calculators, and small handheld devices.*
>
> *That all changed with the development of the notebook computer industry. In 1988, Sharp Corporation demonstrated an active-matrix full-color full-motion 14-in. display using a thin-film-transistor array. The electronics industries now recognized . . . that a wall-hanging television had become a reality. LCDs could be used to replace existing cathode ray tubes.*

If you did not fall asleep, you now know that yesterday's idea of hi-tech is a joke to us now.

You want more? On October 1, 2007, the hand-held calculator turned 40. And in reading all the regaling of this great date, it occurred to me that calculators were the crème de la crème of the hi-tech world just a few decades back, and today's calculators are all 3-D graphing machines. The techiness of a calculator from the 1960s is like an abacus appeared to people then. I mean, a PSP portable is smaller than the first calculator, and if you stare at it for a bit, you're going to realize that it's not really very hi-tech. It's a video player with a much brighter hue.

Everywhere we look, there's a hi-tech this and a lo-tech that. Heck, even Sesame Workshop's TMX Elmo is a hi-tech version of a doll that's been out since today's adults were toddlers. And it's being touted as the ultimate technological revolution. In the next decade, when Elmo is featured in toy stores as a hologram or a virtual friend, that TMX baby will be but a relic. And nothing will be considered technologically brilliant anymore.

Blog
Anonymously
and Lose
Your Self—er,
Your Cell

TREND: Technology is fine. But in the decade to come, it's going to get harder to "get off" on new gizmos.

H ere is a list—imagine, a list—of everything you will need to remember in order to keep up with the so-called new:

1. Social networking is just a lot of hooey. So, big deal. A lot of corporations have figured out that all they need to do is plop up a Web site and make it perty, and we will fill it up with our fondest desires and snazziest wisdom. Yeah, when Home Depot asked me to comment on the "nasty hoe" (my

word choice) that I purchased, and to visit its Web site in order to talk to "the community" (the store's choice), I had to stop and consider that Web 2.99 had arrived: the cheap seats for Web 2.0. Web 2.0 was how this all started: smart-ass Internet companies realized that content is expensive, and that if participants talked to each other, they'd probably forget that no one was doing anything *for* them; advertisers love Web 2.0 because, as in the early Net days, they haven't got a clue, so they think it must be working. Circa 1997, Citibank announced a community for folks to share their stories online (as opposed to "stand on line") to talk about . . . their transaction? It all started then.

2. TV watching is now quaint. I see a lot of the same programming, but it's a lot of work for me to turn on a set and tune in, so I, like you, seek out *The Office* online. What's going to happen to the networks? They will stand on the edge of a cliff, hoping that dumb advertisers will keep shtupping us with 30-second commercials. This is a "last one in the room turn off the lights" scenario. It still boggles my mind that I see *Grey's Anatomy* on ABC.com with three 30-second ads, and yet when I'm forced to watch it live, every few minutes the network breaks the drama for me to watch a douche pitch. It's a little incongruous, and a lot annoying. Yet no one in TV-Ville wants to do a thing about it, and the little gimmicks "NBeeC's Bee Movie TV Juniors" was an NBC commercial, sponsored by Ford, hosted by Seinfeld, and about as patronizing as it was moronically titled. will not keep us tuned in. This is an example of people with small minds who are desperate to make us watch something, somewhere and make us think it's content. I had to laugh when Seinfeld was quoted in *Entertainment Weekly* saying something like, "I asked the Marketing and PR people if these were going to be annoying—and they said no." Who the heck's going to tell Mr. S. he's annoying and hope to keep his job?

3. The fact is, blogs are nothing but online diaries, and most folks who post comments ("memes") do so without using their names. And I thought "crank calling" was illegal! The idea of a post that isn't true to who you are kind of defeats the purpose of a blog. My own definition of blogging: "I speak, therefore I'm interesting." Whenever I see an Anonymous tag, I immediately snort, "Loser!" The refusal to be acknowledged is a sickness that must be stopped. To all of you "anonymities," I beseech you: Get Off the Web. If you have nothing to say in your own name, say it to yourself, because you're wasting precious space online.

4. "Say something once, why say it again," went the Talking Heads with vervy precognition. And yet found information is the reason that most dot-com news or knowledge sites exist. In the next decade, people will start to question the validity of sites that copy other sites that copy other sites. And in the end, the one with the most originality wins!

5. Cell phones are purely toys, as I've said a few times in this book. But what's going to shock you all is that, finally, after our fingers start chafing from all the SMS that we did for years, we're going to learn the art of talking once again. Rest assured: the first phone that promises a clear signal no matter where we are on planet Earth ("dropped calls" are not the issue, Mr. AT&T) will win out. And yes, it will be a Japanese model. Her name will be . . . Dokomo.

6. Off Your Chest 10: I have always thought the Web was about interactivity, but so much of the activity is just people clicking like they use the remote control. The Thrivers Anonymous is something that will start in the next decade as an antidote to all the 12-step groups. There's nothing wrong with support, but I've yet to see I forecast that some cookie will exploit our new cheerful selves as a reason to begin. a

place where people go to talk about how well they are doing in a world they've created. No, we don't need anything from anyone. We merely want to say hey! And meet others online who feel the same. And clap them on the back too.

7. Research, not content, is king. (See chapter on "Living with Ed.") Welcome to the new human-run search engine. I'm privy to a lot of business models that make no sense (see my forthcoming play or book or poem on the dot-com mistake titled, "It's Okay to Sell Shoes"). I've noticed a trend away from "algorithms"—fast speed by which machines find us stuff as we search the engine—toward something seriously cooler, infinitely more intriguing, and finally run by humans instead of a bunch of people sitting under headsets in Costa Rica. For instance, see ChaCha.com. This is not your father's Google. It is also the only time in the book I'm going to reprint from a site in its entirety. I need a break.

About ChaCha

Tired of search engine results that aren't even close to what you're looking for? Us too. So we started thinking about a better way to search the Net . . . and we figured out what was missing . . . people.

That's how ChaCha was born. The first search engine that uses the brainpower of really smart people to find anything you want on the Internet.

I'm back. ChaCha is one of a mere handful of sites that is so smart that even its advertising partners are hand-chosen. For people who are born media junkies (if you're a trendspotter emeritus), a human's beats a machine's find—any day of the week. So, let's ChaCha. Where we join the real world as opposed to being one of a billion getting their "results" from a cold apparatus.

Whither AOL ("Annoying Outdated Leftover")?

A little over 10 years ago, I wrote the following words that are now true. Back then, I was annoyed; today I'm—beaming. "In the summer [of 1996], America Online Inc. admitted it had overcharged many millions of buyers and agreed instead of paying its users the money it charged to give time to them . . . on AOL. If you took the time you waived the right to sue the company for any billing or false-advertising issue, like in ever!"

Now, after changing its business model for the umpteenth time, AOL is finally becoming a dead duck. Back in 1999, when it was all new, the company had many millions of subscribers and a Web site (aol.com) that sat there unattended. I remember going there once, and I thought, "What's this?" It was just a blank page with AOL's logo on it. It was only in 2005 that AOL began to use it as a free site to log into and get a host of ad-supported activities . . . for free. But it was too late, as the company found out, and before this book went to print, thousands of people were being laid off as the company moved from its berth in Virginia to the ad capital of New York, New York.

What does this mean for 2011, you ask with a grimace. Well, first: it all stems from people getting out of the shallow end of the pool and realizing that being patronized (as this company has been evil in doing for a decade and a half) and made to feel not as smart as the rest of us on the Web is not fun.

All right, it's not that simple, is it? Like many corporations, AOL had to deal with a parent—Time Warner, née AOL Time Warner—who wanted it to try everything at least once. Didn't your Mom and Dad want that from you? TW felt that its expensive offspring should go with the all-e-mail-all-the-time crowd, the community bunch, and the free sites model. This kid was not very popular in the end because it had in fact alienated all the other children, who had hoped that one day it would grow up and teach them how to fly on their own. This was the bully on the block who wanted to get away with everything once.

Caught you! From now on, entrepreneurs and corporate Hench-types will know that it's not right to try to fool an entire population that will one day catch on. The jig is up, and a *New York Post* headline said it all when discussing in late 2007 the near future of the company known as AOL, which the Post dubbed "Any Other Label," 'cause no company wanted to claim it worked with the big A in its current incarnation. In this sophisticated, let's-figure-it-out-ourselves society, it's no longer seeming great to treat your customers—or your clients, in the case of companies as unyieldy as AOL—as dumb, mindless clucks who'll buy anything bright and labeled in corporate colors!

As they (yes, we) say in L.A., the guy serving you coffee could one day be the boss of you. Reference outdated, duh, but I have remained true to *They Might Be Giants*, the poor man's REM!

I end this sidebar with a nod of explanation to regular readers: I will not stop until AOL goes the way of Netscape—buried, forgotten, book closed.

Now, don't shut this one.

The End of the Beta

You Just Got to Stop This Affair

TREND: In a society where we *know everything*, beta testing is no longer viable. It's hooey—let the new product loose on a public that is with it not being perfect.

A few months ago, I decided to find out if beta testing, once thought of as the perfect opportunity to just try something out, had become another phrase *sans* meaning. After all, Gmail has been "in beta" for years and is no longer doing much research and development besides marketing the crap out of itself.

It's kind of like a play being in previews and never having an opening for years, which incidentally keeps the critics, who somehow go to shows only when they are invited (cheap bastards), away. This happened in the 1970s when *Beatlemania*, which I happened to sleep through one dark evening as a teen, played for three years without ever leaving its preview period.

Real beta testing is done to keep quality assurances in place—and scientists will never stop testing products until they are done. The days of keeping everything under wraps so that you can fine-tune and twiddle with the damn thing, pretending to be creating while all the time getting members and making money, are a thing of the past now. Why is constant beta a bad thing? Good question. I'm jealous. I have to finish this book one day, and after that, it's on the market. No one should have the audacity to stay pregnant forever!

Adobe, the maker of Acrobat, recently did a beta for its CS3 product, which was implemented the way any tech company might do it. A limited number of users were granted access. Feedback was given, bugs and glitches were isolated, new user-requested features were added, and all was right with the world.

This approach, say my tech-head friends, is always taken for a reason. Namely, despite the expertise of the developers, they can't foresee the unforeseeable. Well, that makes sense. In an absolute beta situation, the program is tentatively introduced to a select population so that feedback can be elicited. This group of users will, based on sheer numbers, encounter greater diversity and frequency of glitches and errors than a single development lab could, with a staff on ready call.

What the scientists regard as general usability and workflow is crucial to the system. Regular dudes can make recommendations regarding new features that appeal directly to the users—period. Developers get a "user's-eye view" of the new application—without the liability of introducing an unfinished product to unwashed you and me. What's more, this is a demonstration of one of the first commonly implemented uses of what the nerds refer to as crowd sourcing.

What's that? The centuries-old practice of outsourcing projects too large to be completed efficiently by a single person or organization, recently amplified, accelerated, and enabled by the unerring power of our friend the Internet.

So Adobe does it well, stops the beta, goes into kappa, which means it releases the product widely, and then starts the product's voyage to market.

To stop the madness of excessive beta testing, a new site was deployed that is going to see to it that companies cease "staying" in soft launch. Invite Share (inviteshare.com) is the first of what I imagine will be millions of sites like it that will make sure that nothing stays private for long. After all, once you get an invitation, you are given entry. In this day of digital communities making money by claiming they are only a test site, a company whose biz model says "In Beta for Years" will soon be in big trouble.

Back to crowd sourcing. This community of testers is what you could call a nirvana situation, creating the product from their own worldview.

CrowdSpirit is a quite ambitious project that aims to utilize crowd sourcing to develop and bring to market tangible under-$200 electronic devices (MP3 players, digital cameras, game-controlling devices). Community members decide what the product is, from concept to design to technical specifications, by submitting and voting on product and design ideas. Winning ideas then get funded by the members of that exact community—and after prototyping and, yep, beta testing, the completed products get delivered to market.

As a postscript, let me just tell you that carmakers have for years toyed with their loyal customers with "You build the car." In Sweden, as a marketing gimmick, Mothership Saab's Brand Center once paid a well-regarded group of prominent Swedish ladies to create the perfect automobile and show us what you want in one. This idea got hyped in magazines throughout the world—particularly since some of the inventive ideas from these gals were doable doodads like soft door covers and, if I remember right, a protruding device so inserting petrol's a breeze!

Slick Saab neglected a beautiful prototype. Never got *on* the drawing board.

part five

ENTERTAIN YOUR DIVERSIONS

"Seriously, Just Being Nominated Is Enough"

Ah, Bullshit, Award-Show Overload

TREND: We start giving ourselves more pats on the back than we give to performers who really are just there to shimmy for us, as we are now realizing more than ever before.

Let's say you go to work, like me, and at the end of the year you get an award for doing your job. Silly, right? Wrong.

That is what the self-servicing (sic) entertainment industries do: give awards for best film, music, TV, book, magazine, and hairstyle (okay, not that).

Hello, and welcome to the awards world, one that will soon go away. This year it's being brought to you by—well, everyone!

It usually happens in January, when entertainment groups consisting of no more than 200 people who were appointed by some politically inept process randomly select the best of last year's crop. Strangely, it's usually the same overhyped products that get all the groups' awards. Funny that.

And it's a big moneymaking enterprise, involving sponsorship and hype and a lot of people paying to be part of the process.

The awards biz has grown by leaps and bounds. The trend is that every organization wants to, or rather *must*, be the first to handicap the best film—or predict which blasé song is going to be the one that [fill in the year] will be recalled by.

So while televised award shows are fabulous opportunities to see our favorite singers and actors, doesn't it seem that every time a performer is on TV, you just saw him telling the same joke or singing and talking his way through his latest product? In 2007, I was shocked—not *Casablanca* shocked, either—to see Chris Rock appear on two award shows making the same lame joke about former Mayor Rudy Giuliani: "Rudy in a crisis is perfect—he's like a pit bull. It's great if somebody's breaking in your house. But if they're not, then, you know, the pit bull might eat your kids." Even the cool are swept up in awards mania. It's like a disease.

Could it be that the people who appear on those shows actually have an album or movie or book or surfboard line that was only recently released? Let's pause to see how much of a wink rather than a contest these programs are. Otherwise, you'd still hear "The winner is" instead of a wince-inducing "The Oscar goes to . . ."

I have nothing against the good works of people who sing for their supper, but gosh, I never got an award for being best CEO of a veteran public relations company. If I had, the tribute would have embarrassed even self-recognizing me! In the near future, as real people begin to get their due in awards of merit for being funny or formerly fat or just possessing good business sense (thank you, reality TV), good work will get the tribute, and award shows will start to seem as silly and pointless as, well, award shows.

Let's make a pact: we decide right here and now that all writers and all filmmakers and all kazoo players did their job really well. They'll get letters from group leaders who will tell them: "Hey, good job!"

What does the best mean now, anyway?

When it comes to liking something, one person's opinion should matter more than a well-researched collective huzzah.

If you liked this essay, click on the rainbow-colored ribbon found on the tiptop of Laermer.com/iloveyou! It's one bomb quiz.

THE GAME OF FAMOUS

A CASE STUDY THAT IS FAR FROM HOLLYWOOD

TREND: Fame is morally neutral, so learn how to be more famous than ever before, or you are going to fail at gaining attention.

"Fame is morally neutral."

—*Edward R. Murrow*
who used to sleep with Deitrich

No matter what your career, hobbies, or interests, if you want to move up in this world, you need to prove that you're successful, that you're the best at what you do. Hard work and dedication can get you watercooler kudos from family and colleagues, but people won't pay you because they love you. To become a top player in your field, you need to achieve recognition, respect, and even notoriety—the mixture that means fame.

Pretty soon you won't make it without being "good famous." That's the kind of fame that a consultant or service provider needs to have in order to let the home (or work) audience know he or she is one of the top practitioners in the field. In sight, in mind. You want to be the one people always consider when they need services or products like yours.

To be fully famous in the 2010s—and take notes if you have a pen or Bluetooth keyboard—you have to create, maintain, and manage a public image that you can, as much as possible, direct and control—you might even consider a fame coach, which you can sign up for on Laermer.com/coachme.

You will be called upon to achieve a position where people come to you because they know you're the best; where, when they're looking for someone in your line of work, people have heard your name, and the idea of interviewing or hiring you seems . . . just natural.

> If you're simply navigating the currents of life, trying to create a satisfying career, you are going to find that you need recognition to bring you opportunities you haven't even dreamed of.

If you're working for a cause, fame can help you publicize it and bring new supporters to the table. If you're pounding the pavement selling a product (like yourself!), you need people to know that you're the only expert on that product *even before you open your mouth.*

In short, in the future you will be your reputation—and nothing else matters. You could invent serious mind-blowing, life-changing, seriously affirming new devices or cures or solutions, but if you're not really well known, it will be hard or impossible to sell them.

Businesspeople looking to advance their careers—and hobbyists, artists, artistes, butchers, bakers, and candlestick makers alike—are about to be thrust into an odd era: one in which "You talking about me?" nets the answer, "Why, always. Yes."

Let me give you a perfect example. A guy named Mike Shullman is the ultimate entrepreneur, not famous but sure on the way to getting there. He owns a series of Minute Man car washes in many towns on the Eastern seaboard. And he takes his notoriety *very* seriously. It's not enough that he's good at advertising Minute Man (he has in fact managed to emblazon his gorgeous slogan,

Clean, Shiny, Dry and Fast ...
...Everytime!

on his stationery, his car, his window at home, and many other ingenious places); he has also become an expert on the car-wash industry and the chemistry of car cleaning. He's the person anyone in any of the media calls to find out a fact about car washes—he's made sure of this by sending e-mails and snail correspondence to anyone who might even consider being interesting in covering his oddly stated "art."

Mike studies every facet of the business around the world ("Did you know that it's illegal in Germany," he innocently remarked, "to wash your car at home?"). He speaks in local communities at forums and in civic meetings, emphasizing his learning and expertise. Result: Mike is taken seriously as a potential mogul and someone who knows his washing, and his local reputation is that of being a man with an expert dedication to his job. He appears to know absolutely everything one could know about something that no one else has bothered to study: what chemicals work best; what car washes in different countries do; what the new and interesting cleaning techniques are. He's the guy you go to if you want your car washed by *the* expert. Oh, and the people in the towns his car washes are located in love him for such ceaseless behavior.

Mike could be beaten down by people who think he's a service pro doing something we should do ourselves and is in fact taking advantage of our laziness.

Ah, fame. It comes and goes like the wind. So we need to ensure that we repeat our message to all the right people—our way.

What happens if someone does something embarrassing? Mike rises above it. And if someone does something bad, he promptly apologizes. This is how reputations stay aloft. The beauty of it is that the news hook may simply be that you cope well under pressure, or that you apologize when you do things wrong (despite being ultra-busy and successful), or that you're a really fair person and nice to do business with.

Remember when Ashlee Simpson was taken to task for lip-syncing on *SNL* and the entire reportage, instead of condemning her, says, "It's a commonly known but rarely spoken about" practice? Simpson is now reputed the world over as someone who rose above this commotion, who was dignified even when she was treated unfairly. Note: I'm fairly certain the whole incident was planned, since producer Lorne Michaels spoke about it a few days later on a strangely-timed profile on *60 Minutes*.

You don't have to be an expert on anything easy or even tangible. Prof. Hann Kari of Helsinki University of Technology has gotten himself known as an expert on disaster! He is even called the Technological Mr. Doomsday. It is pure fear that keeps people in his grasp: Kari will tell anyone whether they ask or don't that the Internet will "bug out" and collapse in an untimely explosion in around 2009. We don't agree here at 2011 Central. He sends out regular releases warning of the technological Armageddon ahead.

This man is tireless in his efforts and stays on message. The result? Kari is the most requested European professor to speak at technology conferences. Are you surprised?

Let's end the chapter with some thoughts—would you believe a list?—on how to be an excellent expert:

1. Talk a good game and be consistent.

2. Make sure, like people know you are a coffee "addict," that you have a specialty that no one else is as up on.

3. Get out there and be on the prowl. It's awful to be loud and pushy, but you kind of know already that self-promotion is the key to success. Conceited. Show-off. Braggart. Arrogant. Egotistical. You forgot one: the successful person whom everyone goes to for a straight answer and who nails it. No, you're not a big Hollywood star on the walk of fame, but in these days of super-self-acknowledgment, you'd sure better act like someone who is.

You're dismissed. Get some fame.

AND THEY
ALL LIVED
HOLLYWOOD
EVER AFTER

TREND: In the near future, we will be happy with celebrities who are more like us and less fake about their lives, particularly about making us believe that they are a couple when they are so obviously just out to promote a damn movie.

I imagine it's hard to be in a meeting with Jake Gyllenhaal. The guy's "red hot" in Hollywood as I write this, and yet he's really not a star. I mean, he was fifth in line for World's Sexiest Man in *People* magazine—and he's a lot younger and better-looking than Matt Damon. Why is it that Jake is not really that big a deal? His image is wayward, and his movies—except the ones that starred the end of the world (*Help! New York Is Melting!*) or the late Heath Ledger's penis (*Bareass Mountain*)—always fail with a thump.

The problem will persist as this young man becomes less well known in the years to come. He'll always be remembered as a guy who "pulled a Tom Hulce," meaning (my words) that he let his handlers take control of him rather than just do it himself. Tom, as you may recall, was Oscar-nodded for *Amadeus* and then pretty much disappeared. I'm positive he was a victim, and a talented one.

Celebrities are now going racing downhill—and you are to blame! Or to thank, I suppose. Today it's already happening. When people like Gyllenhaal are uncomfortably "matched" and then "seen romantically" with actresses whom they certainly aren't dating (Reese? Oh yeah? You need *some* chemistry to fool us), we begin to turn thumbs down on movies where the pseudo dates happen only during the release window. And even though the magazines then gamely show him going in and out of places without her, since sadly they're "on the outs," we, the suspicious home audience, are getting wise to these ploys. Plus, it's so darn telling that he's hiding *something* when there are two obvious gossip column items about him trolling for—it's not young ladies; then seen at a public parlor having his eyelashes dyed! which in combo means he must hate the handling of his career or he'd never be caught in these places! Either that, or he's insane. Oh, and he's definitely the "Toothy Tile" blind items in gossip Ted Casablanca on E! Online. Not to mention the fact that he and also-single actor Austin Nichols were caught, uh, naked, in an SUV behind Chin Chin (Chinese) restaurant and brought into a West Hollywood police station for clothes questioning. Yes, McGraw-Hill legal eagles, this is on the record. . .

What happens to people like Mr. Gyllenhaal is that people in Hollywood and people at home stop taking them seriously as actors. And the problem with Jake G. is that he's actually quite a good actor—in small character roles like those he played in *Donny Darko* and *Moonlight Mile* and even *Bubble Boy*. Soon he will fade out because he isn't anything that we can connect with. He's not a movie star, not a family man, and not even interesting. In a 2007 interview, he was quoted as exclaiming how the scariest part of his job is "answering tough questions from Letterman."

That's not the image a strapping movie star wants to project. So what is?

In the 2010s, we will become more enamored with celebrities who act like us . . . who, because they have no choice, share their real lives with us. I'm not saying that actors in the closet will be that open, but Rupert Everett sure threw that door open a bit—and he still plays meaty roles. It's not merely whether a star is gay or hetero; does he bite his nails, worship his tropical fish, speed read, date midgets with auburn hair, hate intimacy?

With technology that keeps us in touch with them, celebrities will begin to talk to us about the experience of being celebrated and less about how they were snapped canoodling with a costar they didn't meet until just before *that* photo shoot.

This will happen (you need to follow the money again) only when the realness of celebrity—witness the largesse after TV stars on *How I Met My Mother* and *Grey's Anatomy* went openly such-and-such and explained why with glee—starts to sell more than fakeness does.

And so the newer stars won't have to concern themselves with their image, since we'll be right there with them, forging it for them. We'll do blog posts and comments—like Mariah and Britney do now. We'll have our own dialogue with them—and so what if it's their handlers writing it, at least it'll have to be more than an "Oh gosh, I'm so tired of being famous" kind of ego-inflation nonsense that the smart populace is bored with.

With that, thousands of Hollywood publicists will need to be retrained to become technologists. That's a seminar I'd pay to be a fly on the wall at.

Serial Lifer

TREND: Serialized or chapterizations of books, TV, and movies are thrust onto a generation that refuses to give too many precious moments to a single piece of entertainment.

During the first half of the last century, much of what was featured in magazines and on the radio was serials, like the Hardy Boys and Nancy Drew. This was much of what audio theater was famous for. People sat around the fireplace or a bathtub of whiskey and listened in. Then this died out swiftly with advent of TV's blue rays. Strangely, you see these characters appearing every few generations. Nancy had a hardly realized film outing with Emma Roberts a couple of years ago, and the Hardy Boys are back in 2008 with, of all people, fake smiling Tom Cruise and Ben Stiller.

With this attitude toward serialization so ingrained in our minds, you won't be surprised to find that the chapterizing of books and audio/video will be the newest entertainment gimmick in the coming decade. The new adults of the 2010s are more intrigued by bits and pieces—call it short attention span, call it their own understanding of how little time these stories are worthy of at one sitting—and there will be big money to be made by the businesses that pay attention. Did I mention: tiny university classes too?

> The fact is, young people want their information in small sections, like they want their learning and their friendship and their grapefruit.

Well, the last is anecdotal! But they don't have the time to read an entire book at their leisure, and even bigwigs like Amazon are selling by the chapter now.

New "digital ink" companies will release IM versions of books, and they will come with all the bells and whistles known to the Internet kind.

And, of course, you'll always have the micropayment processes of any smart online company that sells you an article. These services are numerous already, but in the coming years these articles will be sold for, oh, a nickel.

At this scribbling, video-learning firm OneminuteU.com and others like it have launched cleverly with every kind of knowledge for those with short attention spans. I love the mere thought of learning *anything* in 60 seconds—since none of us has more than—what *was* I talking about?

On the horizon are ways for you to watch for real—think of live porn, only with some pass-along—and see classes as they happen. My PR firm was handy in 2007 in the launching to the mainstream of lecture capture, a type of absolute university that is kept courtesy of technology for students in the near/far future.

Radio will never do the serialized dramas in our lifetimes because it is afraid to do anything that's not already called hip. But television has already started to do so, with the introduction of something called the clip-ad. It appears for a few seconds as a form of televised theater, but it's really an ad. Online, the short-short redos of series from the 1970s like *Charlie's Angels* and *Rockford Files* into brief 30- or 60-second mini-dramas prove the point that no one needs to watch a plot unfold.

Let's also not forget that music is something we get "on the go" too. Short songs, particularly if they have an odd riff to them, are now more popular than ever; G-d forbid that a newfangled Steely Dan or Led Zeppelin rolled out a three-minute jazz and rock guitar solo, respectively, on the airwaves today . . . nice try.

The funny thing is, popular devices like MP3s (iPod won that war) have actually ruined music for many of the artists who coasted for years on their mediocrity (see the chapter "Mediocrity . . . "). Many lame songwriters and crooners saw their work as something to sell, as opposed to any artistry—producers whose songs had no lyrical value and only some semblance of melody loved the digital era because, well, there were no lyrics to read and everything was upload this, download that. How much credence is anyone giving to anything, anyway?

Thar's the rub. Almost anyone with a digital player reads the *title* of a song. When Queen Mariah's songs all say "Gimme" or "What's that," or any decent rap singer constantly throws punches at a competitor via the name of a song, it gets tired quickly. When the name of a cut is laughable, guess what gets laughed at next?

It doesn't matter how short your song is; your title cannot hide from constantly glancing eyes.

Jennifer Lopez's Antics

The J Down Lo

TREND: Just who does she think . . . ? We are folding our arms and realizing that everything certain celebrities do is bullshit. This cannot continue. After all, the next decade will be brought to you by the generation who invented hype!

As we move from mediocrity into a decade of fabulous, forward-thinking, show-us positivism, we'll always remember the star from the 2000s who turned our cynicism into a beloved trait, none other than J. Lo "Don't Call Me That" Lopez.

People who work in media, like you, constantly shake their ink-stained heads over the antics that any Hollywood figure will engage in to remain in the news. For instance, did you know that Tom "Roseanne's Ex" Arnold, to promote his latest movie, let *People* magazine know—horrors—that he had a low sperm count and it was "killing him" that he wasn't able to have "our own child" with his bride, Julie. And they divorced a year later after his movie tanked, when she probably realized his sperm count was not the lowest thing about him—baby-making skills notwithstanding.

In the 1930s, megastars of the studio system were focused on the buzz they could get from having children or talking of some charity they were sort of involved in, and this most likely culminated in 1960 in the mother of all such campaigns: Elizabeth Taylor's desperate quest for an Oscar for *BUtterfield 8*, which if you've seen the movie on Turner Classics, you know was desperate even for Taylor.

In that moment in time, Taylor portrayed herself as someone who was near death (not in the movie, but in the press, so keep up!), and voters felt so bad that a major star could have kicked it that they gave her a Best Actress award.

No matter how outrageous the gimmick or how much the fake support for the rainforests may seem to anger the masses, filmgoers the world over still will always need objects to worship. And the next decade will not change that one bit.

Larger-than-life figures provide us a service. Love them, despise their hair, chuckle when they hook up, hate them for being rich, but in the end we always plunk down for their offering.

Until now.

Thanks to Jennifer Lopez, people in the media have decidedly had enough of "image a day" puffery.

This woman has tried everything—no exaggeration: she's been a diva, a movie star, a romantic comedian, a put-upon daughter, a lady from the Bronx, a married "mama," a half of a Hollywood duo, a disco starlet, a *Chiquita*, and my favorite: the next Gloria Estefan. She even was sort of pregnant for a while in 2007—coyly denying it, then claiming it at a concert where her nearby husband swore, half-kidding, "We'll go away now"—and yet by milking her prepregnancy it helped to heighten a national debate that did not work; she sold hardly any of two CDs that were rushed out (Spanish-language, then pop). She and Anthony were having twins—no pun apparently intended.

It was probably her 2003 Bennifer Show with former movie stud Ben Affleck that lost her the opportunity for true Elizabeth Taylorhood. During their time together, they pretended *so diligently* to be in love that even people who normally eat up this stuff got a little nauseous over their antics. Watching *Af-Lo* on *Dateline NBC* talking up their evenings preparing meals together—when they looked chemically like they had just met—as a moment for the cookbooks: it was there that their PR camp must have realized it had taken things too far, because in the coming weeks, as Ben was "caught" at a Vegas strip show after cameras were sent a media alert . . . their tearful breakup gave Jennifer a little more time in the spotlight . . .

Then Lo disappeared for nearly two years, only to try three new images (Jane Fonda sidekick, married-to-her-teenage-sweetheart, and ultimately "Call me Jennifer now; I've matured"), all of which bombed.

But in an outrageously long paragraph, it's time to consider what this means for Hollywood in the future. Whereas Jay Low used her fame in the most ridiculous way, The Affleck Chronicles were only one example of her roller-coaster antics: J. Lo Blows were as follows: moaning about abusive childhood memories for her role as an abused wife; being from the Bronx for the tall tale *Maid in Manhattan*; and finally, ironically, the victim of media hype for her underestimated tour dates ("my first time on stage!") with husband Marc Antony. Credit where it's due, though: remember the 2003 Britney Madonna Lip Lock on the base-level MTV Music Awards? It was unveiled that Lopez was supposed to be the third set of lips but bowed out, claiming that retakes on a film were due. She told a reporter later that she (not her

words) didn't want to be the butt (sorry) of any more national jokes, which any Trendspotter knows is impossible, since that's her trade. others have taken to being a little more honest about who they are. I appreciated the new star Topher Grace (Eric, the red-headed kid from *That 70's Show* who hilariously played himself in *Ocean's Something* before becoming a typical star on the rise) saying to *Parade* magazine: "I just hope I don't screw this up, because that's the kind of guy I am." Even if it's faux, you feel good hearing something a vaguely regular guy would say.

And there is something to be said for people like Lopez who think they are G-ds in fact getting a comeuppance from their fans. Overexposure has killed many a career in every trade. In 2001, J. Lo was the biggest of the big, and is now the star most likely to be found soon on Trivial Pursuit. And her album of 2007, *Brave*, was, uncannily, called Worst of the Year by *Entertainment Weekly* for a "too shallow (even by Ashley Tinsdale standards) offering without at least a smallish window into her soul." Finally, La Lopez was made ridiculous by pretending to be an artist on the covers of most magazines in 2007.

She has received only mocking references in one chapter during a book about the future. Who is worse? Well, in 2003 alert media watchers noted an item in the tiny right corner of *Vanity Fair's* cover that portended the future of that one poor lost soul: "Bonus. No Britney Spears Interview."

part six

Make Media Your Friend

(Then Make Bank)

WATCH
AND LEARN

TREND: Perhaps comforting, though true: the prevalence of moving images as our primary means of conveying information will never be going away.

Our relationship with the blue-lit tube began in the late 1930s and has progressed to a full-blown love match.

We left our soul mates—the radio, the book, the conversation—in exchange for an average viewing time of three hours per day, per person (in the industrialized world).

While three hours seems like a trifle, Robert Kubey and Mihaly Csikszentmihalyi, the authors of the 2002 article for *Scientific American* "Television Addiction Is No Mere Metaphor," say that those three hours are half of our total leisure time per day. Let's compare that with the average ten hours a week of "quality time" that married couples share—which, yes, will often be spent in front of the tube. The television is a consuming, though harsh, mistress.

But what drives this whirlwind codependent romance in the first place? In the *Washington Post* article "The Eye Generation Prefers Not to Read All About It," 17-year-old Cecile Guillemin was quoted as saying that she doesn't "have time to read books." And in a hectic modern world, aren't we all thinking the same thing? Isn't the television just one more tool in the race against time (or a tool to save time, glass half full)?

The faster the socio-media information cycle goes, the faster we need to internalize the data comprised in it. Which raises the question—how can we possibly keep up? A cheeky response, true, but if a picture is worth a thousand words, a video stream can be worth a million. Our need to always stay on top of the constant downpour of information leads us to forget about taking 15 minutes to read a thousand words or listen to a radio broadcaster, and instead take a moment to glance at newsreel footage.

But another *Washington Post* interviewee, Craig Patterson, says plainly that he is more concerned with the aesthetics of film over books: "I really don't like reading a story. I like seeing it. . . . I almost always prefer the movie version of a book. Movies can capture the beauty of an image more than books can."

Despite the disenchantment Patterson's remark has caused hundreds of English literature teachers across the states, the works of Kubey and Csikszentmihalyi suggest that there is a more deeply rooted phenomenon at play that explains Craig's overwhelming preference for viewing moving images. This phenomenon is known as the "orienting response."

Pavlov coined the phrase back in 1927, using it to describe a phenomenon seen in his famous drooling dog that involves the "sensitivity to movement and potential predatory threats." Pavlov also called this the "What is it?" reflex.

Kubey and Csikszentmihalyi describe this as "our instinctive visual or auditory reaction to any sudden or novel stimulus." Scientists Byron Reeves and Esther Thorson began to study the effects of the video-editing features of TV on viewers (think edits, zooms, pans, cuts, and sudden noises). They discovered that these techniques directly activated the orienting response in the viewer. Reeves and Thorson state that moving images like TV programs "derive their 'attentional' value through the evolutionary significance of detecting movement. . . . It is the form, not the content, of television that is unique."

Dafna Lemish of Tel Aviv University has shown that even babies as young as six weeks old demonstrate an attraction to the sights and sounds of the television: "We observed slightly older infants who, when lying on their backs on the floor, crane their necks around 180 degrees to catch what light through yonder window breaks."

Our bond with the box begins young.

At the end of the day (that's around 7:45 p.m., when prime time oozes into our being), the source of our preference for viewing moving images over other media—that is, whether it is to save time or because of the orienting response—may not matter. With video footage set to become even more ubiquitous with the advent of mass file sharing and YouTube-type sites that we spend time developing as we watch, more study is needed to further assess the impact this medium has on human physiology, and by extension society.

What's left of it.

The Black Eye of Memory

Media and Big Stories

TREND: Now stay with me. The media will always do what's put in front of them, and that means that until now, the people who remembered didn't have a public forum. Thanks to Web contraptions and our own never-ceasing ability to tell a story with a beginning, middle, and end, we can keep alive what matters, and remember that the true tales are the ones that people lived, not the trifles being observed.

I was on the toilet in my New York pad when the 2003 blackout hit that big town. It was an eye-opener—once the lights went back on. See, I saw firsthand that dark August day how much the media drop into single-line descriptions, no matter how much background (crucial stuff) there might be to a news story.

Sweltering in that tiny loft, I realized how little we'd learned from the truly horrific blackout of 1977. Since I had 29 hours to ponder this, I recalled that fateful day when New Yorkers acted . . . badly. And yet on that notable twenty-sixth anniversary (it's

America, so every year's an anniversary) of the first time I was holed up, I was shocked that no one in our media world cared to remember what had really happened!

August 1977 was sure strange: Elvis had maybe died, and one darker-than-ever night people started throwing bricks and bats through appliance store windows (nothing to do with Elvis). When the lights dimmed, I was working as a clerk in Crazy Eddie's down in the Village. Luckily, in the record store in the back, no one wanted to rob us! Who needs to hear Stevie Winwood in all that heat?

While I was stacking Steely Dan *Aja*, the city just shut down. The town was dark, and the stockroom in the back was even worse.

In those days, before CNN whoring, the lights going out was covered in a laissez-faire manner because no one knew what to make of it! And New York was already in near ruins, with garbage piled up in the streets, police doing the walkout thing, and a high crime rate unimaginable before then.

In 1977, the newspapers had a huge story. So I waited, budding news junkie that I was, to read about it and hear it on my transistor AM (that's a radio).

I didn't hear anything that I recognized. No one wanted to help us; New York was an island unto itself. And yet at the time I got, "We're all in this together." Really?

Back then, our cries for help and coverage were ignored, and our nonregulated electric company had no contingency plans for what might happen if the lights were, say, to go out in all five boroughs. When it happened again in ancient-grid 2003, it was a smiley adventure for New Yorkers, who mostly handled it with grace and verve. But why did no one in the press reach back to 1977 to talk about the pockmarks that once covered the town's now upbeat face?

Lots of New Yorkers held B.O. 1977 against the city for years. That doesn't play well in today's media's nonstop moving-forward-with-the-world coverage. It's not great to remember a time worse than now when people didn't dare to sit on stoops and down beer. While friends tell me that we lit candles, loaned flashlights, helped the elderly, and held a sort of communion in the streets, my friends are romanticizing that long summer evening. We stayed inside and dead-bolted our doors, waiting.

This time we did it: actually assisted each other every which way.

In the seventies I saw people at their ugliest. You don't forget rocks flying through windows. I hoped that people would recollect that you can't be too careful, ever.

Our fabricator, the *New York Daily News*, exclaimed that 2003 was just like 1977! Yet I want to remember blackouts for what they were—what the press needs, and fails, to do with big news stories is not get caught up in a moment of fake revelry. Hey, there was a time when we were not well behaved, when this town was at a standstill beyond recognition.

I ran to ask reporter acquaintances whether they thought we could learn any lessons from these divergent events. They claimed that going back to the history of 1977 didn't make for a good story. Some said it came down to an ugly fact (not fair): "How does it compare to the memory of September 11?"

In theory, I am grateful that New York does have encompassing support from our government. But I would like to see the media practice news coverage the way it was taught in the old days: find the story that is happening; don't just put your finger in the air and say, "Wow, so that's what *other reporters* are saying; it must be true."

August 2003 hit me hard. New York, my former and constant homeland of the heart, is more beloved now than it ever has been, particularly since the attacks, but that might not always be the case. One day the whole country might turn on New Yorkers, and another president might tell us to drop dead, as Gerald Ford supposedly did. That would force us *Ich bin ein New Yorker* to become wolves in the streets.

The beauty of August is always when there is no looting or half-cocked behavior. Still I wonder, wistfully: will there be a day when people go running for bricks again? And how will the media tell that tale? It's something we all need to be cognizant of when we "pick up the paper" each day and see the agenda laid out on our table.

> Let's not allow anyone to paint us a picture just because they like the colors.

News has the ability to change us. It's not just a story to sell papers or get ratings. I think that as those "citizen journalists" rise in importance and TV news becomes a quaint triviality, investigative journalism will rear its head again and be something that everyone will salivate over. You know what that means? It'll make someone money.

Unspun: My "New Media" Is Really Agenda Combined with Ego

> With due apologies to Rod Serling, the news media are nothing but a dark road that has been so well traveled that it feels much like an experiment.

If you take the news of the day and hold it up for a hard look, eventually you can see how transparent it is. In different words, you get to "unspin" it and see who's behind it—who gets something from an appearance in the press, and why so much is put over on us, the media consumers!

We live in a world of hype where the news as reported has more spin than a basketball held on one finger by Meadowlark Lemon.

Celebrities are privately hell-bent on exposing so much about themselves, only to publicly feign distaste for the game—please explain. Is it money? Or is it glory? Explain, then, why a few handy people show up all the time as they gently fade into, "Who was that again?"

- Why do politicians tell us they're about to "go to work" on something that's blatantly unfixable?

- What's the nonnews of the week and—hello? How did it creep into our consciousness?

- Why do anniversaries for nearly anything get celebrated publicly ... and how did it become so easy to become the *first* at something in modern America?

- Why is there so much spinning madness and such a short attention span with regard to news itself? Is it magazines selling what we allegedly want, or vice versa?

And when you deconstruct the news, what is there to find? That everything is about the latest, greatest, and "most known." Friends of mine and I have always wanted to start a magazine called *Best Known For: The Magazine about Death*, but no one has bitten because, sadly, past achievements are a big "you got to be kidding" to publishers.

The world needs to stop the ball long enough to read the label and see where the so-called information was created. To connect the dots lying just beneath the surface, you need to know that most information comes not from sources who proffer it because they wish to "get the story out" (or are prodded to do just that), but rather from those who are paid to make sure the world knows about their latest glory.

Who, then, is the little man standing behind the curtain shouting, "Hey, ignore that little figure behind the curtain"? He is the publisher, who gets, like Murdoch, Zuckerman, and Sulzberger & Co., to say what he wants to say and about whom, what, and where. It's a game. And it costs us our worldview. I mentioned ego at the beginning of this diatribe. And since conglomerates are "top down" in tone, you can imagine what the News World, *US News & World Report*, and the New York Times Company ask of their workers: to put themselves more into the story and align it with the goals and mission of the Corporation above all else.

Coverage? I guess so . . .

Bending facts to mean something that's less than factual is the stock in trade of the news publisher. And with five companies owning much of the media these days, it's a simple chore to think about *EW* and its incessant raves for HBO's underperforming *The Wire* as if they were owned by the same conglomerate (they are). And what is Viacom's relationship with Paramount, which owns DreamWorks? How come *Fortune* has written so few negatives about AOL? In the early 2000s, I helped a reporter pal at *Fortune* concoct a long story titled "Where Are They Now?" about failures from the just-gone dot-com days. She informed me, "I was told no way to touch anyone at AOL."

Have you noticed that people say the funniest little gems about things they know nothing about? It's disturbing that the person I live with cares *nothing* about Hollywood and still asked: "Did Brad really throw her out?"

It took my breath away.

Certain folks are always visible—and the reason why is unfathomable. For example, Aston Kutcher is always in the news. He always has something to say. AK said a few months ago that he'd be back in boxers as a model if his new movie were a box office hit. He made a bet that he'd return to his former job if his new movie was the weekend's top grosser. It was. And this was news, too—major. He told TV's *Access Hollywood* that in the same forgettable flick, he had a nude scene. "I like being nude. So, for me, it wasn't incredibly tough."

Welcome to headline news in the present. Sure, everyday people talk a blue streak on the air about what some of the news means. But wow, try to look through it. How does it become newsy or watercooler talk in the first place? Well, you need a fourth sense—an ability to look at the "fourth estate" and see what's being fabricated so subtly or sometimes blatantly. Because, you see, all media provide entertaining anecdotes for interested parties to absorb. If you really *get into it*, you will see that the person being quoted is there for a reason. News is a consumer product just like all the others; it's created by someone, for someone, with a single goal in mind—to make a profit. News has been romantically made to be something more than that, and as someone who has been paid to do just about everything in media, I've got to tell you, there's a lot put over on the media consumers!

The superficiality of the press needs to be unspun by your own eyes! That means that you go deep into the discussion rather than just sitting there—internally digest and comprehend the media that you look at. Yes, the media were once places where people went to get dependable knowledge from trained experts. Today they're bent. The folks gathering the information are not trained or mentored, and so they run from "source" to friend, all of whom in essence are trying to turn that space that you read, watch, and listen to into a blatant sales pitch for product. In often-used 1990s words, not that there's anything wrong with that. It is, however, crucial that you own an arsenal in order to be savvy about what's being presented to you.

You need to look beyond what people report to be real news. Someone whose internal antenna is alert to these phenomena used to be called a news junkie—someone who can read it all and get why a company was featured in a story that it really had nothing to do with.

Do you know how bad it is to read what you want to? Do you want to be boring—the world's greatest crime? I, for instance, read *Prison Life* magazine, and it gets me a lot of needful information, as does my poring through *Call Center Digest*. You have to stop reading the same old things. Stretch, or st—r—e—tch. It's good for you.

Is this the absolute longest sidebar you've ever read?

The point of the matter of the fact is to be someone with a fourth sense. Use tools to get more from what some call "the fourth estate" and get to the scheme of what passes for news! What with media growing from a handful of places to everywhere you turn and with everyone a published reporter, thanks to our friend, the Web, you have to be careful about what's pretense and what's not.

There's no better time than this decade, during mediocrity, to become an educated consumer of media fodder. Understand it before it takes you over. Believing what you see every day in the paper is no longer viable— or a healthy practice.

Be a creator and a promulgator of the *un*spun mentality . . . get to the root of every story Was Katie Couric told by her bosses to cross her legs that way on her very first day? before you get any less cynical. In the end, your reporting standards are probably higher than theirs.

THE MEDIA NEXT DECADE

TREND: The press will stop being meaningful because, well, we know more than it does.

So we're all journalists. Woo-woo. But why can't the "regular reporters" get with the program and stop being so proud?

There isn't a single reporting method to which each of us doesn't contribute—

Yet, with few exceptions, you won't get an e-mail back when you correct and/or add content to a story that was run in a regular newspaper.

Here's the problem: the media are scared *sans* shit. You have more time on your hands and may be better paid than the ink-stained men and women who, once upon a time, were the ones we looked up to for information.

Yet local newspapers, and particularly the dailies that believe in informing the public, as opposed to showing off (the *Desert Sun* of Palm Springs is an excellent example), have no qualms about telling you how to find the perfect lampshade—in a sidebar, no less—and explaining why a particular street can't get rid of its potholes. When I read this "small" paper, I discover such common-sense (Voltaire said, "There's nothing common about common sense") educational tools as how buds regrow on flowers and why certain cements are harder than others. And yes, I care.

But with mobile info-gathering abilities getting better by the second—thanks to Radio Shack and cheapie sites that offer technology by the boatful—our blogs, podcasts, vodcasts, cell video, and even SMS typing skills mean that we can report on the latest happening before any weekly, daily, or even minutely reporting agency can.

I often look for the day when committees of media companies will take a big step forward and start really giving us the help we need. Case in point: each week, the Circuits mini-section of the *New York Times* offers us a look at the latest whiz-bang techno-freak device. But it never gives you a way to buy it. Why? Because that would be advertising, the media dudes are always saying. But so what? Isn't the point of the press to make it easier—and as for any kind of scruples, please! Do the people at the *Times* think the company's stock is dead in the water because people still think of the *Times* as the Newspaper of Record, rather than just a good place to get the latest gossip from the world of business (something at which it excels)?

Take a look at monolith Time Warner's *Southern Living* magazine as the example to beat the band. Sometime in the 1990s, it began to run ads and editorial in the same space—the first major publication to say the heck with it, let's just find out what's "Southern enough" (I said that), make money with it, and give readers the goods. That magazine is thick, and no one gives them shit for advertorial regularity.

Also, during the Mediocre Era, a major media writer at the *Los Angeles Times* wrote a fabulous article stating with blunt honesty how you could e-mail him, he guessed, but under further investigation, the fact an address is featured under his articles is just a device. What he said, shocking to read, was that this is merely procedural, and he has no interest in getting back in touch.

To tell the truth here and now: media people are high and mighty. Their perch is about to be kicked hard. Like the *National Enquirer* has been doing for decades, all media will begin to pay us for our scoops. If they use them, you get a few bucks . . . and the satisfaction of knowing that information is in the pen of the beholder. The fifth estate, perhaps?

Hey, they had their chance, and any honest reporter (of which group I was a full-time card-carrier a few decades ago) will admit that he or she blew it with self-importance. Long live the phone mobile camera operators. We like to watch.

part seven

THE LANGUAGE
OF LIFE

ONE POTATO, TWO POTATOES LATER

TREND: People will try to change the language and get nowhere, since we're stuck on calling ourselves funny names.

My, oh my. What would have happened if the potato farmers had made it impossible for us to say "couch potato"? To show how ridiculous and humor-free people can be about pop culture terms, I posit the best example known to this book.

Potato farmers in the United Kingdom mobilized to stop the term *couch potato* from existing—they wanted "couch slouch" to take over. As Chef Anthony Worrall Thompson (who was behind the effort, which was unsuccessful because "slouch" is like "tsk"—a word that no one wants to use publicly, mostly because it reminds people of their mother's advice), explained:

> *Potatoes are one of the UK's favourite (sic) foods. Not only are they healthy, they are versatile, convenient and taste great too. Life without potato is like a sandwich without a filling. I am more than happy to get involved and bring goodness back into the word potato.*

Goodness! Who said anything about low-carbing our way off the potato island! Gee, this kind of politically or socially *earnest* correct behavior will not continue into the next decade. Here's a laughable reason why.

In 2005, members of the British Potato Council (BPC) and other potato industry leaders petitioned to remove the phrase "couch potato" from the *Oxford English Dictionary*.

BPC marketing manager Kathryn Race was quoted in the *Farmers Guardian* (a real magazine, read by unreal people): "[Couch potato] is defined in the *Oxford English Dictionary* as a person who takes little or no exercise and watches a lot of television. This is a derogatory phrase that misrepresents potatoes, a low fat energy source and an excellent source of vitamin C, all essential for a healthy diet."

Then Conservative MP Nigel Evans puts forward a motion calling for the phrase's removal. And finally, they all fight Robert Armstrong on the floor of Parliament. (Who's he?)

And then the people of the U.K. stood up and said—and I do not quote—cut the crap! There was an outcry to behave like decent British people, and in America, where there is a story about every single "fad" known to humankind, this one didn't even make the Associated Press, which hires people to do "Weird and Notable" stories every day. Potatoes are just a food. Couches are a place to lay your weary hiney. And finally, in the end, well, this is the end of this chapter.

WHERE ARE THE PHRASES TO CATCH US?

REVIVAL OF "FUN SPEAK"

TREND: It's time to bring back catch phrases so that we can say something better than "It's hot" or "Dude, you got it going on!" to one another and smile with the memories when we're old and dodgy.

Cat's meow. Horsefeathers. Drugstore cowboy. And one I heard as a child, that was sung to me whenever I wouldn't leave the bathroom: open the door, Richard.

They were playful. They were colorful. And they were how we spoke. Before the 22-minute sitcom laugh track robbed us of imagination and a discerning ear, back in the era of arty comic books and quick-witted radio plays, everyone alive expressed themselves in an idiom that made conversation vivid and lips curl. When World War II servicemen plastered "Kilroy Was Here" doodles on walls across Europe, it was only the latest example of the era's endearing colloquialism. These old phrases were not even politicized. They didn't have to be profound, or be spoken by a colorful gal like Nell Carter!

Kilroy's being "here" was so much more luscious than anything clever that Mr. ("Gosh I'm quotable") Clooney or Mr. ("I'm da decider") Bush could say. During World War II, says the lore, Liberty ships were being turned out very fast, so much so that one inspector working in a Boston shipyard, a man named Kilroy, would often find the proper people and papers not available for him to sign. Thus he scrawled on many a bulkhead—and we mean thousands—just the words "Kilroy Was Here."

Okay, so there was no more war in the mid-1950s, but we all looked to charming and lovable folks like Lucy and her kooky relatives. The next decades were full of extraordinary national and global change, but we still found time for quirky language that was good for a smile. These terms occupied a sizable portion of the TV-watching vernacular. We talked about bee's knees, getting sozzled, and seeing you in the funny pages! Phrases managed to exude folksiness *and* modernism.

Now they're missed sorely. I don't care if Snoop Doggy Dogg thinks his throwaway lines are catch phrases 'cause they're in fact a lot of breath spent on nothing. And lines from the movies these days are meaningless (You had me at what now?). Ah, but the movies give us one amazing catch phrase icon.

Midway through *The Big Lebowski*, Jeff Bridges's character, the Dude, feeling his way through a typically addled description of events, refers offhandedly to "the parlance of our times." While his specific reference is to the phrase "trophy wife," the line, like much of the movie's dialogue, is made funnier by the casual relationship that the characters in TBL share with both language and reality. The "times" to which the Dude refers are the early 1990s—September 1991, to be exact, if one notices the date on the $0.69 check he writes.

Ask someone to rattle off the fashions and fads of that month, and you might conjure up as many images as for September 1971 or September 1921. But parlance? One strains to recall phrases from that long-ago, sepia-toned era of Arsenio Hall and the Gulf War that match the vitality of earlier generations' everyday language. ("Don't have a cow," perhaps?)

What makes "the parlance of our times" such a perfect little gem for the Dude to drop like a breadcrumb during his verbal meanderings is that it sounds like a turn of phrase he might have heard somewhere else and absorbed, subconsciously, into his own vocabulary.

It wouldn't be the first time for the Dude. A television shows the first President Bush warning that "this aggression will not stand." The Dude repeats the phrase a few scenes later. Another character uses the word *abide*; later, the Dude does too. He is as much a receptacle for words as he is for White Russians. Were the film steeped in 1990s vernacular, he'd be an ideal recycler of its nuances. But what the movie demonstrates to us is the *paucity* of contemporary idiomatic flair. The movie—among the most quoted and quotable in recent memory, threaded with language as colorful as its characters—is tied strongly to a *where* (Los Angeles), but not necessarily to a *when*. It's a place where an anachronistic term ("coitus") is more memorable than any modern equivalent.

Aside from language borrowed *directly* from the technocultural zeitgeist—after all, Googling yourself may *sound* snazzy but it's corporate *shillery* (that's the only time you will ever see me italicize *three* words in a single sentence)—more organic additions to our jargon seem inauthentic. If anyone writes me saying "Let's hug it out bitch" is a catch phrase, I'll smack him virtually! Like everything in our accelerated media universe, one that is chiefly concerned with selling as quickly and as broadly as possible, quirky language often feels forced. Postmillennial lingo like "off the hook" and "bling" might be as vivid as their Jazz Age counterparts, but they also derive from a fickle, consumerist youth culture that sheds its old skin twice a month. Modern slang is usually guaranteed to have a short shelf life as relevant/vibrant.

Our language's stultifying mildness is a single-fixated by-product of our media culture's stultifying cautiousness.

Speaking colorfully often means speaking with spontaneity, and spontaneity equals danger. Politicians, celebrities, athletes, and broadcasters—anyone in a microphone's way—all tend to draw dutifully from a shallow pool of publicist-approved clichés. When a public figure—be it Dan Rather or Dennis Kucinich—infuses his message with some colloquial pizzazz, it is certainly conspicuous—and derided. Phrases can't just be silly or folksy now. They have to be tactical. Focus groups must gauge how well they sell detergent or Democrats. The results are disappointing. We may have a sound-bite culture, but the sound track often calls to mind elevator Muzak.

Now I feel the Phrase is on the return. See, our clothing is being retrofitted to make us look like we came from another era, and our music is turning backward into the sounds of the 1980s. Why not language? The moment will be ripe in a bit. After all, digital democratization and viral culture supply the tools for a new wave of Kilroy-style phrasemanship. At long last, we have a loosening of the postwar era old media's grip, a surge in user-created content, and an endlessly expanding sea of niche-oriented expression. It is a time of electronic graffiti. Voice mail, e-mail, text messages, blog posts, YouTube auteurs—everything is aimed to grab attention instantly. Colorful language that paints a picture with an economy of words should be of exceptional value. The year 2011, even more than today, will clearly be a year defined by those who can provoke a response—even a chuckle or a smile or a double take—with shorthand. Old-fashioned phraseology can definitely play a role.

How does the Age of Idiom sound?

Feel the Verb

Something that happened from the 1980s to the 1990s was that brand names entered the mainstream as generic words. From FedEx to Google to TiVo, a whole mess of nouns developed out of the sheer magnitude of buzz.

Then came verbing.

Googling was huge for this type of activity, particularly after it appeared on *The West Wing* Don't White House staffers use the FBI to do background checks?, followed by a whole bunch of others like TiVo that hit our mouths so naturally. Then, the first-timers who used a DVR before it was understood couldn't think of a bona fide way to describe the phenomenon.

Quick! Fast-forward to the 2000s, where this is no longer plausible. The fact is, the noise level is too high, there are too many places to look for words, and besides, no one cares about brands. We simply don't need to. We'll go with whatever's the handiest or coolest.

But back then it was pretty wild for branders. NetFlixing was having videos sent, eBaying meant online auctioning, and even a smallish online service called Kozmo was in the vernacular as Kozmoing instead of one-hour delivering! My firm was sort of responsible for that—it launched the media boondoggle that was Kozmo(ing). This happened because, heck, we were just totally zonked by whiz-bang. The actual product didn't count for much.

That doesn't happen today—not even with the giants. Now we live in a jaded world, where the noise level is too high, everyone's competing for our attention, and no one is loyal to anything fantastic anymore.

For instance, even if another scandal were to happen, "doing a Monica" would never exist. And I think that even if a fashion trend (Flashdancing) were to start today, our attention spans would not handle any more descriptions. Even the term *Paris* (slang for shallow) hasn't caught on. And if you need more examples of losers, keep score.

First, if fast food fails to turn any constantly repeated words into vernacular expressions, you know what that means. There's hardly anyone alive who doesn't know who invented the phrase "finger-lickin' good" to excuse the greasy mess that KFC cooks, and Taco Bell has tried for years to get people to buy a "fourth meal" (fourthmeal.com) as no one dug in. Even now, Starbucks, which runs the world, isn't really a verb—nor is "the third place," that living room environment it failed to pervade in a massive way.

Three second cousins, YouTube, MySpace, and Facebook, are huger than Jesus' disciples, but none of them is anywhere near a verb—and you do not think of them as verbs because each is faddier than the other.

(Facebook does come closest to being a full-fledged trend. I appreciate how it grew up from being a college home to something that everyone I know is at least trying. It's e-z. And, yes, *2011* has a Facebook thingy replete with its own futuristic and pretty ingenious widget—and our own Fun Wall, natch.) In our follow-up, probably called *2016*, YT, MS, and FB will have morphed into nonthreatening pals. All but one has a Daddy, and Facebook has a sugar daddy—and that's what happens, as always.

Epsonality is what bland Epson wants us to actually possess when we shop for copiers, while Dewarism is a failed way of getting drinkers to ponder definitions of drinking (as if we needed more).

On NBC, neither the hip TV outing *30 Rock* nor the ratings giant *Grey's Anatomy* opposite it could get people to pick their shows up as verbs—and yet both share "vajayjay," a cute and acceptable term for vagina that's widely used. Hardly anyone knows where it derives from.

Some verbs *have* worked, but they won't be filling anyone's pants pockets soon: U.K.ers talk about Chunneling, but it has naught to do with the trains and more about the structure—after all, we're not Aerostarring or even Acelaing for the high-speed train in the United States. And Airstreaming, for you trailer freaks, breaker-breaker, has not worked its way into mainstream trash talk!

People have really stopped trying. It only causes trouble with smart consumers. For instance, if you are "being JetBlued," it means being stuck on the runway!

Arg.

Fun footnote: I hear people "Full Frontal PR"-ing their stuff these days, and I'm told that a "Punk Marketing" is a strategy, but I'm not conceited enough to think that either is sticking, except in my own overactive brain!

TAKING
RESPONSIBILITY
FOR YOUR WORDS
IS NOT JUST GOOD PSYCHOLOGY

TREND: In the future, the people in charge are going to say, "Enough with the spell check," and everyone is going to be responsible for the work they produce (or don't bother showing up).

Question: Why can't people be careful when mistakes are only going to make things worse for them?

Sure, you heard your parents mumble that one time or another. But I'm talking about writing. Almost everything I read has errors in it—and not because Grammar Check has lost its magic. I see a lot of carelessness coming from people who believe (I think) that somehow someone else is going to make the document perfect.

Who is this someone else? Typos are mistakes *you* have to catch. While everyone makes minor goofs, I see major ones all day, and they're unbelievable. I'm here to ask every marketing professional to take a third and fourth look before hitting the Send key or printing on super-fancy paper.

Some say it's the fault of e-mail. That sounds like a big excuse coming on. People pass their documents back and forth and add rather than correct. Since I am part of the last generation that once used typewriters and rejoiced at the invention of Wite-Out, I place the blame on those large monitors on our desks. There's no way you can catch a boo-boo onscreen, but most folks won't print out their written work. It's too much bother.

Today, work product travels casually from desk to desk until the work goes out without someone realizing, "Wait, wait. That's supposed to say *aunt*." (That's a private joke for *Curb Your Enthusiasm* fanatics.)

I am a kind of typo savant. I see them out of the corners of my eyes. As a matter of fact, my mate and I live part-time outside L.A., and we laugh at crazy errors in "cable ready" Time Warner ads constantly. I see them in staff and management reports—I was born a proofreader—where folks create documents using the wrong words, or worse, being grammatically incorrect (GI). If an author doesn't even bother to use spell check, I know that he or she is simply sloppy.

Recently I have come undone on seeing some doozies that found their way to me from unexpected sources. Witness:

LA *Times*. For the last month, there has been a front-page Cars section advert that is nearly a quarter of a page; it actually says, "LOVE WHAT YOUR DRIVING."

Re/Max calendar. I got it in the mail—no mean feat because it was octagonal. It was printed with verve and style. Problem: the proud real estate professional calls herself "YOU'RE DESERT REALTOR." (Yet I'm not!)

South Florida CEO magazine. Here I bought a frame; this was so delicious that I wanted to show it to everyone who came into my office. Anyway, this particularly bad example calls John Murphy (who knows) the man behind MURHPY'S LAW.

Read that twice. In case you haven't seen it, this periodical is glossy and expensive.

Showtime. In announcing the first episode of *The L Word*, the words blaring onscreen spoke of the upcoming PREMEIRE.

I'm not going to get into the incorrect usage of *less* and *fewer* in multitudes of costly print ads, nor the occasion a few years ago when the *New York Times* ran a Sports Friday section on Saturday morning.

Uh-uh.

I have to talk about Arkansas here because no one bothered to proof there. If you pay attention, you'll do well on the quiz (Laermer.com/words).

The 2007 law stated: "In order for a person who is younger than eighteen (18) years of age and who is not pregnant to obtain a marriage license, the person must provide the county clerk with evidence of parental consent to the marriage."

That meant that in Arkansas in 2007, it became possible with parental consent for, say, a 10-year-old boy and a 9-year-old girl to become husband and wife, or a 40-year-old man and an 11-year-old girl, thus granting them state permission to engage in sexual activity regardless of other laws on the books making such activity illegal.

This was a big crisis for the state. It was possible that pedophiles from elsewhere would rush to Arkansas, pay some horrible parents a few dollars to gain their consent, and "marry" a child—legally. Arkansas's legislators and governor found themselves in a strange spot. The lawmakers meet as a unit only every second year, meaning that a remedy had to wait until January of 2009.

Then there are books, since most are edited in what appears to be committee-speak, as if the editors group together, all talking haughtily about plot or mise-en-scène or arc. The copyeditors are jokers hired more for their knowledge of the people who work at publishers than for their ability to eradicate dangling participles.

There's a Fnord in this chapter too. I want you guys to be thinking about the book you have slogged through here. Nonfiction works are *usually* merely about the phrases everyone can use at cocktail parties (like, er, *Blink*). And no one really reads them, even if they buy them. And if you're reading this, you will notice the typo on page—I'm not going to TELL you. But gosh, most of them have so many mistakes. Last year I read one called *The Middle Mind*, where a biggie publisher allowed well-known words like *Schrek* (sic) to be misspelled. The subtitle is, "Why Americans Don't Think for Themselves," which means that *Middle* is open to criticism.

A few years ago a fairly cool *idea* for a book on how companies steal corporate secrets contained so many made-up words (Exon, as in Valdez) that I had to put it down. Editors don't feel like taking the time, even if that's their job, I guess. Yes, everyone must take responsibility for the words in books, I hasten to add selfishly.

All that cash is lobbed at voluminous printing and giant ad campaigns and expensive promotion and oft-appearing marketing, and what does it do in the end? It turns people who notice errors right off. In cases like mine, products or parent companies are never purchased (from) again.

I definitely make mis-steaks. Yet I don't trust my undercaffeinated self, so I hand my work to others who see me with a critical eye.

Don't people fear ridicule? Not during the era of blamelessness.

> These are days when people say, "Yeah, well, I have a reason" and refuse to accept a scintilla of fault.

Think about this the next time you hear someone exclaim, "My bad"—an overused phrase developed by a generation of underenthusiastic mini-thugs. It is iconic of the age. A guy won't say, "It was my fault," and can't admit, "Oh, I'm bad," or, heaven forbid, apologize. Instead, he's coining words gently to make fun of the fact that he screwed up. Ha, ha.

I'm not trying to be all Joyce Brothers here. I just like to read, look up, and watch TV without observing typos that stop me cold.

To some, this sounds like bellyaching or preciousness. Yeah, let's live by Apathy Rules: giggle and say whatever. But being careful and slow is in order during strange times: see the economy go haywire, a wartime president who is seemingly unstoppable and bizarre, and our entertainment written for 11-year-olds . . . why not spend some quality time concentrating on the slippage we produce?

I paraphrase Tony Soprano's shrink in a third-season episode: indeed we are all getting caught up in the little things. The big ones are all taken care of, and so we're lucky; we have that ability to focus.

Dr. Melfi was a genius. We have got it all, and then some.

In fact, life gets sweeter when you pay attention. Regardless of what OutKast says, there's still that chestnut about the roses being smelt.

A long time ago, a guy I respect, but also thought was a bit of a turd, told me in a moment of extreme clarity: "Focus and concentrate. Everything comes together." That's inspiring advice (even from a turd). I'm glad he took time to spell it out.

On Writing Poorly: Singing Out for the Day When Someone Takes the Language Seriously

Can't anyone write? I get it — I've asked a few times — but seriously.

I realize that bitching and moaning about the state of the English language is old hat, but I'm concerned. I work with some of the smartest people I've met in eons, and yet when I look at the lazy drafts I receive—which aren't well thought out and also haven't really been given the attention they deserve—all I can think of is: as an employer, I'll pay big money for a writer who needs zero edits.

I asked a bunch of people on a Web site last year: "Do you have a hankering to place creative, collaborative, and cool words on paper to communicate messages to the world? Then call me. I'm in The Book."

I'm in a service business that communicates on sensitive and timely issues. And yet whenever someone shows me a letter, press release, idea, Point of View document, or memo, it's filled with garbled sentences, unoriginal ideas, and bad grammar.

Without demeaning the people I know—well, I'm really okay with that, so don't write me a letter saying, Oh really?—let's take a peek at the reasons people in the new worker gen, or ages 21 to 33, don't write, in case you don't know why. . . .

1. Accountability is the word, not grease. . . . I mean, someone else will catch the mistakes, and I'm really busy.

2. Words are hard to find; you have to actually stop and consider 'em.

3. Using clichés is so much easier than making yourself sound original.

4. Why bother? I mean, really. If you kind of get what I mean, haven't I won?

5. The truth is (not): "No one reads these"; "The client doesn't care"; "Let's just get it done."

6. Our job is to talk, not write. (That's the funniest one.)

7. Spelling is such a pain. Spell check is hard to use, with all those squiggly lines.

8. The language is easier on IM. Didn't I SMS that to you a little while ago? Why did you not response (sic), LOL?

9. My boss's outlandish expression of horror when he reads what I write is fun to see. It seems to be the only exercise he gets, dude.

10. "I don't need to learn anything, I know it all. Don't I? I mean, Mom told me that."

11. The old farts working here know this stuff much better—they'll have a go at it.

If you think it's frustrating to spend every other minute editing someone else's sloppy work that was done purely to get it done (A guy who worked for me once muttered: "Don't make such a big deal out of it just because it's only sort of good"), then you are right.

On Laermer.com/lazybastards, I've listed in no order the *other reasons* sent to me by people who read what I said and wanted me to know I was not alone.

So now I've decided to retire from what I do for a living—PR—and devote my remaining years on Earth to online tutoring of kids (ages 0 to 29) who really wish to write better. (Okay, look, I've been writing professionally for 27.5 years; I want the language to survive me!)

Get in touch if you want (me) to help. You know, I'm only a third kidding.

Devolution and the Real Language of Life

Devolution doesn't mean the opposite of evolution. It's actually a much more interesting and complex concept that businesspeople had better understand right now. The truth is, devolution is the process of transferring power from a central government to local units. Power to the people, so to speak.

Language is the currency of communication. Anyone reading this knows that without language, we have no purpose. Then why have we federalized language, refusing to acknowledge that the power inherent in language is within all of us?

Take jargon. Most of us don't listen—you are probably supertasking now—and don't talk to people in their own language. So next time you're in a meeting, create a real-life lexicon and *discharge* it with such force that you compel everyone in the room to use the words and phrases you chose. Energy, man. We can develop a lingo and set about making it vernacular. But it doesn't stick when the second we step outside the conference room, we start to talk in form letters—a bunch of words that are brought to our lips because they're what we say every day—and we forget the words that we forged together as a unit!

In politics, devolution creates local bodies to perform tasks that were previously carried out by centralized groups. To protect the value of the currency of language, marketers must cease to behave as Big Brother of words—and learn to listen and speak to our audiences in the patois they understand.

On a planet where verbs are sometimes made from brand names, emerging companies make up words and phrases and then market them as cool, but their audiences have no idea what they're talking about. What's a *hungerifilicious* snack bar, Snickers? Sounds like full-fledged nonsensical sales jargon to us.

Sales people'll do that.

An audience that does not understand you will not buy from you.

Look at McDonald's. Boardrooms in Des Plaines hosted countless meetings (nay, thousands of focus groups), and from these confabs came a global marketing campaign that would cover everything from advertising to tray liners: "I'm Lovin' It." Adorable, yeah, but this campaign has not made us long for a Mac. Truthfully, it's just three more words that say nothing.

In order to shepherd the devolution of language: when you are asked for an explanation of the language in a marketing spiel, replace what is being explained with the explanation. Use plain English (unless you don't speak English, in which case use plain anything).

Listen to audiences without preconceptions. Assume that the words used in your meetings make sense only there. Remember that language is influenced by more than mere demographics. Geography plays an important role. For an illustration of this, try ordering pop in the United States outside of the Midwest.

If you are asked for an explanation, and the explanation you give makes sense, use the explanation and not the language of the life you've lived thus far. It's not our job to hope that audiences are smart enough to hear what we're saying. That's like writing a shit script and hoping the actors will make it better. Because you know the actors, like the people we're selling to, have something better in mind.

LIVING WITH ED

TREND: Your world will fall apart if you don't do research. Mocking you is an art form.

It's not my thing to make fun of people just for kicks—okay, it is, really, that was a test of self-aggrandizement, and it failed miserably. Back to topic: I've got to kick Ed Begley Jr. in the ass.

This younger Begley is an okay performer; I liked him as an innocent on *St. Elsewhere*, and he was pretty nifty as the craggy hairdresser on *Six Feet Under*. He was also on the very first episode, young kid, of *Maude* as a helpless door-to-door dude. And last year I met him at a party in Santa Monica and let me tell you this guy is "circus tall."

At the party, Begley stood above us all with his pretty wife, Rachelle Carlson, straining her neck, and they held court; I listened with a chocolate martini in my hand. It's an L.A. acquired taste. Not enough liquor. I learned that Begley is not a very good brand builder. At the shindig, he was going on and on about their HGTV series titled *Living with Ed*.

At the time I had never heard of it. I'm a fairly well-informed guy when it comes to culture, so I looked it up on Live Search. And guess what? I got about a thousand hits for "Living with erectile dysfunction."

A press release clarifying the show's title appeared a few days later, and I now know that Viagra isn't a proud sponsor of, nor a brand integrator in, the *Living* "problem."

HGTV will introduce a new genre of programming to its lifestyle sched-ule—a docu-soap starring real-life married actors Rachelle Carson and Ed Begley Jr. in Living with Ed. *The six-episode series reveals the often quirky green lifestyle the two share and argue over in their modest solar-powered Hollywood home. . . . The show focuses on Rachelle and Ed's relationship and their sometimes differing views on how to live green.* [No erectile dysfunction issues whatsoever.]

The lesson is: always research those adorable names, and do so thoroughly. Oh, and the people who were "optimizing" *Living with Ed* told me, as an aside, that they spent most of the month prior to the HGTV premiere "trying to get the ED companies to link back to us"—for a sizable (sorry!) fee.

What a world it is to advertise in today, if you're not careful. And particularly when it's so damn easy to do so . . . click and point and say yeah baby.

To Hell in a Handbasket

Like you, I'm trying to figure out if we're in such steep decline that we are going to be tossed away by some G-d up above. So see you, and that'll be it for humanity.

The origins of the phrase "to hell in a handbasket" have gotten me thinking. I wanted to know how such a phrase came into existence.

The "handbasket" phrase has indefinite meanings. It became popular in the first half of the twentieth century, almost exclusively in the United States—not in England, as you might imagine from *The Importance of Being Earnest*, where that little boy was found in a handbasket (Wilde called it a handbag, but then I'm a Coward fan) and society with a capital S was shocked, I tell you, shocked by it.

The first indirect mention of THIAH comes in the *Wichita Daily Times* in May 1913: "and when you won't buy from me and I can't buy from you we'll both go down the tobog to ruin in a handbasket." In this specific phrasing, "handbasket" appears to mean an impromptu sled, one that would quickly speed you to ruin.

But there are other possible threads. Wikipedia, whose democratization of the act of defining makes it a good spot to go for subjective knowledge, suggests that a "handbasket" might constitute a "mocking reference to the Guillotine, which often used a lined basket to catch a severed head"—the insinuation being that the doomed soul formerly attached to the basket's contents was heading, shall we say, south.

A couple of people and places propose that the simplest explanation is also the correct one: a handbasket is a small basket carried by hand, and therefore easily moved about. When something is progressing easily to ruin, it's "going to hell in a handbasket." Language expert Michael Quinion said so. He's an expert.

Then again, as early as 1629, the phrase "heaven in a wheelbarrow" was used to essentially mean go to hell. I guess it's the opposite of the handbasket thing . . . since a wheelbarrow is as difficult or heavy to take anywhere as a handbasket is easy to carry!

Yes. We're all going to hell—are we ever—in a European carryall.

According to *A Supplementary English Glossary* from 1881: "To go to heaven in a wheelbarrow is a euphemism to express going in the other direction. In the painted glass at Fairford, Gloucestershire, the devil is represented as wheeling off a scolding wife in a barrow."

It's all confusing in a fascinating sort of way. Watch when this sidebar appears—suddenly lots of folks will tell me that their ancestors coined the phrase, just as the wealthy and established Benedict family did when its patriarch died in 2007: everyone in the family swore he'd invented the egg concoction as a hangover recipe. Yeah, right. Why hadn't anyone ever said anything about it before? "Because it seems untoward that any member of our family," one Benedict explained, "would invent something to get over a night of drinking."

Dear Reader: Since No One Can Seem to Write, How Do People Show Intelligence?

Spelling is key—we do so much online social networking that if you can spell, you're a genius. It displays a level of sophistication that far exceeds the SMS txt speak that eclipses public discourse. Maybe it doesn't show that you're super smart, just that your writing isn't way out vulgar and despicable.

Then again—"actions speak louder than words" is applicable. Showing your intelligence through action (whether it be via your own creativity or some other modality) may be the latest way of exuding intellect. Or be Forrest Gump: "Stupid is as stupid does."

The sensible way to show your intelligence is by being quiet.

There's lots of claptrap out there, so why not be the one person in your group who ponders? You could be the one of whom they think: "Gosh, man. He doesn't say much, but when he does, those words are golden."

Another way to show you're a smarty-pants (or to demo prowess at data storage and recall) might be by rattling off mindless minutiae like Cliff Claven did with absolutely no aplomb every single G-d damn day on *Cheers*.

Also, if you look at the rise of "hipsterism" (see Cosmo Kramer), it's not so much about being intelligent as about being connected in a way that allows you to rock the latest trends. The more connected you are, the faster you learn of the trend—clothing and music need apply. Your peers can see by the music you listen to and the clothes you wear that you are "hip" (i.e., ahead of that never-ending curve). So the discovery I made in writing this is that hip is better than intelligent now. We are doomed.

part eight

SOCIETY WITH A SMALL "S"

New Rule

You're Not Freaking Cool Just Because You Say You Are

A multifaceted chapter in many distinctive parts with several adaptable products.

TREND: Consumers will look askance at companies that seem like they're cool, but in a sense are just marketing themselves to appear that way. They're fakes.

Being cool doesn't mean saying you are, so stop. It's too easy to feel faked out.

Part of the Apple identity—indeed, perhaps *the* most Apple-y thing about Apple—has been its status as the techno landscape's lone wolf, the fiercely independent brand whose software and computers were untouched by outside influence. Sure, the company was an ego- and bottom line–driven giant, but it had an aura of uncompromising individualism. An aura in which its patrons basked! Its cult grew around the thrill captured in the famous "1984" Super Bowl ad—with our user-friendly, soulful machines we were all smashing the hegemony of those *other*, uncool monoliths, the ones that demanded compliance.

The sheen might be off.

From his tangles with record labels over content to corporate partnerships with places like Starbucks, Silicon Valley's ur-maverick, Steve Jobs, is beginning to invite the type of criticism once reserved for his competitors. A decade ago, Microsoft, the ultimate purveyor of "uncool" software and gadgetry, threw its detractors into hysterics when it decided to bundle its Internet Explorer Web browser with the Windows operating system, a move that triggered its epic showdown with the U.S. government. Critics decried the move as a serious curtailing of consumer choice. But what else could you expect from those stodgy suits up in Seattle?

Well, it turns out you could expect similarly irritating restrictions from their hippie rivals to the south. Heralded as the Next Big Thing from Apple's design wizards, the iPhone was the most anticipated product launch since fire. It would be history's most advanced cell phone. And AT&T/Cingular was the exclusive carrier. Period. Consumers with another service were out of luck. Those who had been hoping for an unlocked phone that was capable of working across networks were chagrined. So much for independence and corporate disentanglement.

Even when it isn't undone by user-unfriendly policies, Apple's cool is finding itself threatened by appropriation. The iPod—the new century's most zeitgeisty, least assailable product—is beginning to prove another age-old axiom: with success comes the inevitable erosion of hipness.

Marketers use the devices to pitch their message. Banks use them to play background music. Schools incorporate them into lesson plans. There may be no triumvirate more apt to kill buzz than marketers, banks, and teachers. The iPod may very well be a victim of its own exponential rise. When the decade began, those cultural tastemakers located on the cutting edge purchased iPods for cachet and cool. As it winds down, their grandparents are downloading the newest Andy Rooney podcast, and the tastemakers must tap their feet expectantly and wait for what's next.

I couldn't understand why my Shuffle couldn't get the words "Get off your ass and join the revolution" engraved on it. I asked. I was told that certain words are unacceptable. But wait. *I'm* the only one seeing it. My Shuffle now says, "Apple Censored This."

And then there's iTunes. Offering me a chance to "complete my album," but giving me a time limit, is surely not cool. An entire section devoted to songs on *TV commercials?* No, you didn't! And finally, the uncoolest cut of all: the fact that I can play my songs on only five computers max, and if I cannot locate which one a song is on and want to deauthorize them all, the system shouts: "You may only deauthorize all computers once per year." Rules—not cool.

They've become the man, man.

Google's unofficial corporate slogan is "Don't Be Evil." It is, one hopes, also the company's operating principle. But as Google's already gargantuan influence becomes still more gargantuan, many observers have begun to wonder whether the elegant, powerful, and still very cool products that Larry Page and Sergey Brin offer might mask the potential for some decidedly uncool privacy issues.

For years, the company's growing stranglehold on the average person's Internet use—first through an innovative search engine that acquired brand recognition that Kleenex and Xerox could never have imagined, then through e-mail, instant messaging, mapping, and most other basic functions—has led to fearful speculation that "Google knows too much."

It loads our browser with cookies that identify and tag our computers. It scans our e-mails for code words that trigger advertisements. It knows where we live, what we like, how much we like it, whom we contact, and for what. The company's acquisition of banner ad Goliath DoubleClick will only increase its capacity to track the average person's online activity. And here is where cool can become something far, far less appealing. While we all love to Google stalk, we hate the idea that it can be done to us as well. And while we marvel at the potential to have every word ever published available and fully searchable, we cringe at the thought that an astonishing range and depth of details concerning our private lives might be available and fully searchable first.

The very omnipotence that makes Google so invaluable has made it a threat. So far, the company hasn't suffered. The brand still connotes whimsy, its unorthodox offices are seen as the model for employee-friendly practices in the wondrous decade to come, and, importantly, what it offers is just too powerful for even the most jaded cynic to ignore.

But because cool is, by definition, ephemeral, people suspect that Google's adherence to its famous three-word pledge might be too. The time might not be far off when people check themselves in the shower for Google's fingerprints. Big Brother isn't cool.

In July 2005, MySpace was the fifth-most-viewed site in the United States and an unstoppable force on its way to gathering all of America's hipness (or youth) under a single digi-tent. It wasn't just a way to network with friends. It was, in our post-Ed Sullivan, post-fanzine, post-MTV world, the new fuel for cool. It played kingmaker in a splintered, Long Tail universe. Sloppier than Google and more interactive than YouTube, it was the vanguard of Web 2.0, a frontier where America's two primary populations—exhibitionists and voyeurs—could not only frolic in symbiotic harmony, but prosper. Just as eons ago the cool separated themselves from the not-so by registering for an online domain, now "see me on MySpace" defined the digital divide.

That month, Rupert Murdoch bought MySpace. Shortly after the deal, Google struck a near-billion-dollar deal to advertise on it. MySpace continued to grow, becoming the third-most-viewed site on the Net by October 2007, although more slowly and with rival Facebook on its heels. The arrival of "el hombre" didn't really *change* anything. It's unlikely that current MySpace users genuinely care (or even know) that News Corp. runs the show now. Nor is it reasonable to believe that anyone looking to network or make friends would look elsewhere *because* of the buyout.

And Americans under 60 are so conditioned to relentless, ubiquitous marketing that even the site's slow descent into crass consumerism is not going to incite backlash.

But News Corp.'s purchase signaled a new era for the site. It sold its unruly youth for a leveraged maturity. MySpace is now, for better or worse, a key cog in a global media empire. It serves as a cross-promotional platform for other News Corp. products. It targets and markets. It's filled with spam. And more than half of its members are now—gulp—over 35 years old. They may have deep pockets, but they are definitely not cool.

On a more elemental level, the site is no longer about what fed its meteoric rise: social networking. Instead, it's like a catalog of the American mediascape, a barometer of the popularity of everything from Mitt Romney to the aforementioned Victoria's Secret. There is very little that's grassroots or underground about anything that most major companies and celebrities now subsidize, whether directly or indirectly.

Then there's Netflix, which I denigrate with a pause, since man, that company had it all. But forget the one lesson that most corporations often do and you'll go down the tubes: success is about being honest. Netflix is not. And I'm severely disgusted by the coolest idea losing it.

1. It makes too many claims and offers and assumptions. It's wince-inducing to see "You've heard about Netflix" on popup ads. What club do you not want to be a part of where everyone on Earth is a freaking member?

2. It dounces (my word) you if you order too many DVDs in a single month.

3. It works with many online companies—some were my clients—to help them improve their online customer service but refuses to cooperate when one of these companies wants to discuss the partnership with the outside world (e.g., the media).

4. It is simply Blockbuster on wheels. Plus, partnering with a major-domo technology company to bring downloaded movies to a set-top box. Gosh, we've been doing that since 2003. Uncool, not new! As I type this, another STB manufacturer goes belly up with *thudtastic* force.

It's not possible to stay cool. It was 15 years ago that a too cool for school type came into my office and said, "Richard, you're so stylish that the cups next to your watercooler are amazing." Today I've got Dixie Cups, not even blue ones.

With that, here are the Simpsons embodying how super-cool can stay for only so long.

Homer: So, I realized that being with my family is more important than being cool.

Bart: Dad, what you just said was powerfully uncool.

Homer: You know what the song says: "It's hip to be square."

Lisa: That song is so lame.

Homer: So lame that it's . . . cool?

Bart and **Lisa:** No.

Marge: Am I cool, kids?

Bart and **Lisa:** No.

Marge: Good. I'm glad. And that's what makes me cool, not caring, right?

Bart and **Lisa:** No.

Marge: Well, how the hell do you be cool? I feel like we've tried everything here.

Homer: Wait, Marge. Maybe if you're truly cool, you don't need to be told you're cool.

Bart: Well, sure you do.

Lisa: How else would you know?

How to Keep Nascent Trends from Dying on the Vine

How to Cope with Change, Too

TREND: With everything going on in our lives, sometimes something stops us—and here's why, how, when, and where it's headed.

Most trends come and go, but some recur like the seasons. Rather than stemming from the vacillations of technology and pop culture, they are rooted in deeper phenomena, stemming instead from underlying elements of the human condition. When describing them to people, I refer to these persistent cultural trends as "perennial" or "meta-trends" Meta-trends force us into personal reflection when confronted by a life-changing event.

Regardless of one's life situation or one's degree of self-absorption, the surging current of life can pull us under and trump any boastfulness. And generation after generation, we invent new ways to mitigate this phenomenon and the reflection that it necessitates.

For some of us, the life-changing event is abrupt and violent, like a soldier losing an arm from an IED in battle. For others, it's like a train wreck in slow motion: a breast cancer diagnosis, then months of harrowing treatment. And then there are those events that do not ravage the body, but are just as traumatic—for instance, people whose homes were consumed by a wildfire (like the fires that hit southern California). But in all these instances, the whys and wherefores of one's life change are evident. It's straightforward as an event that inexorably changed us.

In the examples just given, we are dealt a hand that immediately changes our way of life, and we are humbled by the circumstances that have befallen us (yes, even the billionaires residing at Carbon Beach). Our personal reflection is in response to the change we confront.

However, personal trauma followed by personal epiphany doesn't always apply. Many times, our epiphany steals upon us like the proverbial thief in the night. One day we awake to the realization that although there is no distinct event that we can point to that changed our lives, we've changed. This person, me, is not the same as the one from before. Essentially, realization signifies the "life-changing event" in question.

It might be a buildup of minor events that brought self-realization, sputtering like some old rusty steam engine. Or maybe our awareness suddenly roared to life in the face of a serious calamity. In either case, this is our clarion call to look beyond the confines of subjective self-awareness; existential dread compels us to find out exactly how we should relate when we are presented with drastic change.

> Up to now, we as a society have relied on institutions like organized religion and established cultural traditions to mitigate a meta-trend, giving us a sense of our place in the universe. But these institutions are changing in the face of the increasingly fragmented nature of our pop-infused, media-driven society.

People are now turning to the stylized fanfare of multimedia escapism, celebrity worship (along with its assorted célèbres that we champion), self-help fads, alternative spirituality, and increased fascination with the paranormal. And we manifest the underlying meta-trend further through the continuing acceleration of information technology and the rise of a generation that researches more than we snore.

Some signs of where this is headed are the immense popularity of the *Matrix* series (even the bad ones), preaching its own cyber-saturated rebranding of an essentially Manichaean worldview. I had that look when I first heard that word. It's a theological reference to those movements inspired by the ancient religion founded by Mani, who promoted the idea that Good and Evil (caps theirs) are equally powerful and are locked in struggle forever. Or, the popularity of the *Left Behind: Eternal Forces* book and video, laden with apocalyptic Christian themes. Another sign is the prevalence of people leaving reality behind in favor of MMOGs like World of Warcraft or 3D's Second Life "virtual world."

More examples are evident when people's fascination with and emulation of celebrities like Oprah and Martha and Rachael and Ty from *Home Makeover* are considered. And if fixating on their favorite celebrity isn't enough, people searching for a renewed sense of meaning can choose among an assortment of celebrity causes, like the Lance Armstrong Foundation's "Livestrong" campaign or the charity work of DiCaprio or Jolie. Rather than relying on our own moral compasses, we now only have to mimic our favorite celebrity persona! But it doesn't stop there; the counselors of these celebrities become our counselors. Take Dr. Phil and his burgeoning franchise, or Rhonda Byrne.

Her completely bizarre *The Secret*, with its alchemical themes and spiritual subtext, is the best example I can give you of alternative spiritual paths that even mainstream society has seized on in great, mystifying numbers (another is the widespread popularity of yoga—it's in every single grammar school gym class). Also, our persistent fascination with all things paranormal is evident from recent hits like *Crossing Over* with John Edwards and Sci-Fi channel's *Ghost Hunters*—plus the three prime-time programs with interchangeable names that are all trying to be *Ghost Whisperer* with J. Lo Hewitt. Documentaries and TV shows that explore our fascination with vampires, Bigfoots, and UFOs are oddities offering their own avenue of wondrous diversion to the bemused postmodern soul.

Such phenomena provide us with ways to cope with all the change in our increasingly volatile and tumultuous world, punctuated with wars, catastrophes, and what I call "bolts from the blue." But what forms such meta-trends will take once we've seen the full-on advent of things like full immersion virtual reality and nanotech is anyone's guess. It challenges the imagination to contemplate what cultural trends might emerge—and how we will talk to one another when they do. I for one am up for that challenge.

The future is a calling card for possibility.

LOOKING VS. SEARCHING

TREND: What's with all the online searching—what happened to finding it our own?

We are everywhere, and we are nowhere. Google gallops, Wikipedia whirs, and we have what we need—whatever we need—in a spin of the hourglass icon. We've assembled our digital Alexandrias, shrink-wrapped our memories and our memes, and set everything on the windowsill for our seven billion closest neighbors to see. What we know, they know; what they see, we see. Never before has the success rate for "finding" been higher, even as what we "want" becomes ever more specialized or ephemeral. We want to find the shortest route, the lowest fare, the fastest news, the most toxic commentary, that jingle we heard 20-odd years ago, and an infinite number of material doodads that we hadn't wanted at all until we spotted them right there, linked to that other thing.

That you can "find" whatever you desire in 2011 is assured. You need only look.

Mere looking is not what got us here, and mere looking will not deliver our future. And when we "find" what we are looking for too easily, something is just as quickly lost. Ours is an irony-choked culture, and here's a doozy to choke on: at some point recently, all those search engines killed the search. Once we were a global community, seeking what we didn't have, with our evolution derived in part from a stinging urgency to leave behind whatever plateau—literal or figurative, grand, small, soft, or . . . you get the idea—we'd wandered too long upon.

The big searches, our course, are easy to spot. We crossed the seas. We went West. We took to the skies. We flung ourselves at the moon—a harsh mistress. But what compelled us to search was more elemental. Searching was vital to our human condition, at a time when humans had fewer answers and even fewer text messages. It is still.

One needn't have been a cowboy or astronaut to wonder, "What is out there? Can we find it?" The questions connect us—to our inner voices and to other people alike—in ways that technology can't improve. Nope.

But now our access is too comprehensive, our reach too wide, our technology too powerful, and, well, *your* lives too comfortable to bother with much *genuine* searching. We haven't ceded control of our lives to machines, despite what alarmists and half-baked sci-fi social theory suggest. But perhaps we've reached a point of diminishing returns. Or perhaps we've crossed some kind of digital continental divide, where the energy and focus that once radiated outward now flow into handhelds and headsets, feeding our passive absorption.

Even the very big notions or needs—those that formerly were worthy of a quest—are often assimilated into this culture of looking. We don't search for true love anymore; we sign up and scroll through a couple of hundred faces seeking the hot one. If they filmed *Citizen Kane* next year, Rosebud would turn up in a Topeka garage, and the mogul's assistant would have it shipped overnight. Effective, yes. Better, even? Mm-mm. But mastery and enjoyment are very different, and as we tame our world with greater and greater speed, our willingness to do what is difficult or unorthodox recedes. By making the unimaginable imaginable, we are back on the plateau, content to look around.

> We are a world of lapsed, bored seekers capable of finding anything but loath to discover.

We are more inventive than imaginative, able to devise wondrous tools for looking and possessed of a remarkable knack for "finding," but reluctant to search for whatever lies beyond.

We no longer need to be discoverers, frantic to explore a world that's too big for us to grasp. Instead, we catalog the world and consume it with a few clicks. Our world is a desktop. It's less exotic and vast, painfully unmysterious, and hardly worthy of adventure. When we look for something, it's because we're pretty certain we'll find it. When we search, it's because we ain't got a clue.

Time and efficiency be damned.

> Perhaps it's useful to remind ourselves often that we fall into both camps. Only then will we get what we want.

SAY YOU'RE GAY AND INDUCE A YAWN (OR, "GAY FOR PLAY" HAS HAD ITS DAY)

TREND: In these years, people who come out of the closet to attain fame and fortune will be told, "Been there." The books will remain on the shelves, as we're tired of gay for play.

It's a big gay world out there. At least, that's what the press wants you to believe. From my viewpoint, as a fuchsia card-carrying gay alpha male, every few years there's a boondoggle in gay stories in America: the Supreme Court said OK to sodomy in Texas; Iowa in the heartland says OK to gay weddings; Richard Chamberlain (Richard! Chamberlain!) claims he's a homo; while finally (my favorite) MTV said OK to the air-

. ing of a band (t.A.t.U.) that portrays itself as being "all lesbian, all the time." The mega-ratings grabber Tia Tequila featured a bisexual lady of indiscriminate taste, but I'm not sure if she's into sex as much as she is into showing off her inanity.

Yawn, digress. Is all this really the series of huge breakthroughs the media are suggesting? Because it sounds to me like just a lot of hype to sell newspapers. Truth is, we've seen this all before.

A generation and a half ago, Rock Hudson came out to the world on his deathbed because of complications from AIDS, smack-dab in the middle of Reagan America. At that point, a scant few years before the Supremes said no to sodomy in Georgia, the mass media talked a good game and asked Americans to be a lot more compassionate in their dealings with their gay brothers and sisters.

Then we waited for 24.5 years—past noise like "Don't ask, don't tell," past Barry Winchell's horrific death from homo-bashing Army boys, past that shady Defense of Marriage Act and doe-eyed Matthew Shepard, to, finally, a gay bishop happening upon the scene somewhere up north. So the big news now is that it's OK to be gay. Again.

Of course, it isn't entirely OK. The media message of the moment notwithstanding, Bill Frist, the Republican leader of the U.S. Senate, reacted to gay movement forward by grandstanding that he'd like an amendment *to the constitution* that gay marriage be disallowed.

That is progress with a small "p." Not gay with a capital "G."

So how can we explain this dichotomy? Perhaps the public isn't really so much more accepting and the culture isn't really that much different—just as it wasn't back in 1985, when Hudson died.

> Perhaps the reality is that the media have grabbed onto this story line more because it's a sellable one than because it's the truth.

Let's go back to Chamberlain, whose story says a lot about why people are going "Senator Craig?" (who cares; just go away) as this book is being readied. Chamby (my pet name) has a publicist who insists breathlessly that he should get a big "wow!" for his act of boldness. He should? For 40 years he played dull and, oh yeah, straight. Then he got exciting and on the cover of *People* magazine for telling the world that he's gay. Really? And, oh yeah, he happens to have a book for sale. Which I'm sure is just a coincidence. Much like Liz Smith, who also conveniently came out in what very briefly became a must-read memoir. But don't get me started on Liz Smith.

One day after Richard's big moment, I stood in a trendy Santa Monica video store and spotted the original *Bourne Identity*, which was remade last year with the straight (well, today!) Matt Damon. Chamberlain played Damon's role in the first version, which no one remembers now, since Damon has turned this into *his* role. I had to laugh at the laboriously butch face Chamberlain was making on the box. He hasn't had that kind of fame in years, and his new efforts—retired and notoriously gay—reek of a last-ditch effort to gain a buck off fame.

To make matters smellier, the old boy told *Dateline* at the time that he is "not a romantic leading man anymore and [no longer needs] to nurture that public image anymore." Did anyone in the press ask about his implicit suggestion that his fans are total idiots?

What Richard Chamberlain's old-world PR people were pulling was very 1950s: let's tell the world he's gay to get some more attention. Right. Ask Rosie O'Donnell how far being queer's gotten her, really. Certainly not the lead of *Price Is Right* or a punditry on MSNBC. Chamberlain is an actor who has been downgraded to his generation's Larry Storch. You know, another TV actor who has had to pay the rent by appearing in, say, cheaply constructed bus and truck companies of *My Fair Lady*. Now that he's gay—such excitement!—maybe people will pay attention to him again.

He leapt out of the chartreuse wardrobe . . . and there he is on TV as the new Henry Winkler with good secondary roles on *Will and Grace*, *Nip/Tuck*, *Hustle*, and bizarrely in the big-screen horror show *I Now Pronounce You Chuck & Larry*, called by critics the most homophobic filmed gross-out in years (Richard Chamberlain has morals, yeah?).

So, in my summation to the court: the media are overjoyed about creating circuses around people diving straight into gay-dom, and the courts nod their assent to a bedroom act. My mind wanders back a decade to the Gay March on Washington during those naïve first days of shamelessness (or Clinton I). There, with little fanfare, I saw Martina Navratilova address hundreds of thousands of wide-eyed attendants. Stop looking for signs of acceptance, she shouted with no irony. Acceptance can be revoked. "America needs to see gays and lesbians as just as boring as they are."

Since the generation that invented hype has finally come of age, the 2010s will be a decade in which actions, not bedroom eyes, will be what we seek out in our heroes.

Faith, Politics, and the Death of a President

TREND: We are going to stop being so milquetoast about admitting that people get solace from G-d. It's just a fact. Let's not categorize the Religious as either right or left. People can be more than one type.

A lot of us are afraid to admit that religion is, and will be for a while, what most people stand for in their lives. This came to light during the pomp and National Day of Mourning for President Gerald R. Ford, who was one of the few past presidents who was honored for serving his country so nobly during a time of great crisis.

But while the events surrounding his death, especially the funeral at the National Cathedral, received gobs of media coverage, the funeral was reported as a political event to the exclusion of what it actually was: a devout and unapologetic religious service.

The ethics and humanity that powered Ford's life were religiously based, and in the next decade, people won't cower from showing the way faith-based living defines some people. By covering the funeral service as a rally rather than a time of worship, the news media, including the *New York Times*, missed a golden opportunity to focus on the core inspiration that directed the life and work of President Ford: religion.

A key component of the funeral was the moving sermon at the cathedral, delivered not by a renowned figure, but rather by the Episcopal priest at President Ford's church in Rancho Mirage, California. The Rev. Robert Certain used the Beatitudes from Jesus' Sermon on the Mount, in the fifth chapter of the Gospel of Matthew, to cite positive values for those who love God and serve humanity. Paraphrase from the contemporary English version.

Though beautiful beatitudes, none of this color appeared in any articles or on TV, which surprised anyone reading through them who knew Ford. I knew him as president, then as a revered neighbor in Coachella Valley; his name is on the Boys/Girls Club down the street. As a result, the picture drawn from the coverage was missing the element of context. Faith was ignored, and in doing so, the national media did a disservice to Ford's legacy. This woke a lot of the nation up, who, in later eulogies in the press, wondered aloud why this element of the service was a problem.

And there was one that said, for the first time in this era, let's give higher credit where it's due. Ford always said that his faith led him day to day. To "cover" his life without mentioning his relationship to a nonpolitical power demeans a great man's memory. It is the duty of the press to stop looking to the lowest-hanging fruit in such cases, before such hypocrisy does us in.

609.72, Minnesota Statutes 2006

The Oddest
of Current
Laws

TREND: Laws that small people make are really making it hard to imagine leaving your house, so you think to yourself: "I'm gonna stay home. It's dangerous out there."

609.746, Minnesota Statutes 2006

(italics mine)

Copyright © 2006 by the Office of Revisor of Statutes, State of Minnesota.

609.746 INTERFERENCE WITH PRIVACY.

Subdivision 1. Surreptitious intrusion; observation device.

(a) A person is guilty of a gross misdemeanor who:

    (1) enters upon another's property;

(2) surreptitiously gazes, stares, or peeps in the window or any other aperture of a house or place of dwelling of another; and

(3) does so with intent to intrude upon or interfere with the privacy of a member of the household.

(b) A person is guilty of a gross misdemeanor who:

(1) enters upon another's property;

(2) surreptitiously installs or uses any device for observing, photographing, recording, amplifying, or broadcasting sounds or events through the window or any other aperture of a house or place of dwelling of another; and

(3) does so with intent to intrude upon or interfere with the privacy of a member of the household.

(c) A person is guilty of a gross misdemeanor who:

(1) surreptitiously gazes, stares, or peeps in the window or other aperture of a sleeping room in a hotel, as defined in section 327.70, subdivision 3, a tanning booth, or other place where a reasonable person would have an expectation of privacy and has exposed or is likely to expose their intimate parts, as defined in section 609.341, subdivision 5, or the clothing covering the immediate area of the intimate parts; and

(2) does so with intent to intrude upon or interfere with the privacy of the occupant.

(d) A person is guilty of a gross misdemeanor who:

(1) surreptitiously installs or uses any device for observing, photographing, recording, amplifying, or broadcasting sounds or events through the window or other aperture of a sleeping room in a hotel, as defined in section 327.70, subdivision 3, a tanning booth, or other place *where a reasonable person would have an expectation of privacy and has exposed or is likely to expose their intimate parts*, as defined in section 609.341, subdivision 5, or the

clothing covering the immediate area of the intimate parts; and

(2) *does so with intent to intrude upon or interfere with the privacy of the occupant.*

> So like I said—and you agree: "I'm gonna stay home. It's mad dangerous out there."

This is where we are headed now. Every male in 2007 is afraid to touch anyone accidentally in Minnesota. It's a gross misdemeanor, and a gross misreading of law. What would the fine characters from Coen Brothers' *Fargo* say to this bummer?

"Gee. Gosh, golly, hmm. Ooh. Saints alive!"

For a host of unbelievable laws, log on to Laermer.com/moveout. No quiz, just a lot of stringent headshaking. For instance, did you know that fruit is illegal in New York bars and that until the 1970s, serving liquor on Election Day was illegal? Saints alive! In St. Charles, Missouri, for supreme example placing, there is a new law on the books [soon to be abolished] prohibiting table dancing, drinking contests, and cussing. Specifically banned for now is "indecent, profane or obscene language, songs, entertainment and literature" in bars. Of course, no one has actually explained what constitutes indecent, but I can bet this bill falls under the guidelines. Want additional examples? In Barre, Vermont, there's a law on the books that requires all residents to bathe every Saturday night. State law in Louisiana prohibits fake wrestling. And my new favorite: the state of Michigan pays people three cents to kill starlings and ten cents per crow. These and more on Laermer.com. Go, okay? I'll stop pitching you!

Demeaning the Presidency Has Brought Us Down

TREND: We need to stop pissing on the Leader of the Free World. It's not becoming.

In the last year, responding to a question about President Bush, Rep. Charles Rangel told his television interviewer: "I really think that he shatters the myth of white supremacy once and for all; it shows that, in this great country, anybody can become president."

While that was funny, it's really not. That a sitting member of the U.S. House of Representatives, one in control of the Committee on Ways and Means—and his marbles—would say this about the current U.S. president says a great deal about where we are.

This is far more revealing about the times. Disparaging remarks that once might have been whispered behind closed doors over a cigar and brandy are now broadcast proudly into microphones. It seems like the office of president has been degraded to historic lows.

Will 2011 be a moment of renewed respect for the office or continued ridicule?

My first instinct is to point to the office's most recent occupants as the culprits. "The White House is a shrine to people," said Bob Dole at the height of the Monica Lewinsky scandal. "It's a shrine. I think when things like this happen, people are shocked." If half of the country seethed at Bill Clinton's casual relationship with an intern and the other half seethes at what must be perceived as Bush's casual relationship with reality, it seems likely that most of the damage to the institution has been self-inflicted.

People have lost faith in the apparatus of leadership. Yet this answer is probably insufficient and shortsighted, both of which I have little trouble revealing.

On one level, there appears to be a permanently reduced level of trust. There have always been good presidents and bad ones, but all Commanders in Chief were citizens first, at least in the way they acted. Watergate shook decades' worth of accumulated faith in the idea that a president would not "do anything" to the people, and now a seat of authority and respect has become a man waiting for the next scandal—and then the one after that.

Now when something hits, it seems there's no going back to liking the man—or, one day, woman. Deepening partisan rancor has accelerated the process—everything is a fight these days.

After the Soviet Union's demise, we appeared to have more time to concentrate on a leader's personal failings. So now the office no longer seems like a big enough oak for leaders to scamper and hide behind.

In 1971, the counterculture was cynical. In 2011, the culture is.

Still, in the future, we need to concentrate more on the big things in order to rise above the mediocre center. Here's an example of how not to see the world.

In January 2007, a commenter on the Chicagoist.com blog complained that the editors had devoted an entire post to the passing of Momofuku—and one to the creator of instant Ramen noodles. Yet, said the blogger, there was only a single link mention on the concurrent passing of President Gerald R. Ford (yes, he's in the book a lot). Another post firmly acknowledged that Ford probably deserved more than afterthought status, but then added: "On the other hand, who hasn't eaten Ramen noodles?"

Ford's presidency was forgettable, but it's still tough to imagine Calvin Coolidge being compared unfavorably to dehydrated noodles.

Politics aside, George W. Bush often seems uncomfortably close, in a certain media fishbowl way, to Lohan or Spears or Simpson (O.J.). He is just another very public person whose very conspicuous flaws are very easily identified, very funny to caricature, and very much ridiculed . . . and on a loop, no less!

We can hope to rid ourselves of the tabloid presidency. Consider an analogy from 1950, when the media created and destroyed Marilyn Monroe, yet somehow Dwight Eisenhower remained perched far above the fray. But . . .

That would have been a comfy place to stop, but comfort is not my bag. See, it's not really ever "politics aside." It's impossible to separate politics from a discussion of the degradation of the presidency.

In the current zero-sum climate, defenders of any president will point out any disrespect, even if none exists.

Responding to a long *National Review* article chastising Keith Olbermann for calling Bush "Mr. Bush," Media Matters blog noted that William F. Buckley Jr., *National Review*'s founder, has referred to "Mr. Bush" in the magazine's pages 150 times since the president's inaugural. So in the game of deriding the president of the United States, let's say respect is in the eye of the beholder.

PLANNED LAYOVERS IN AMERICA

AN ARTICLE THAT DID GOOD

TREND: People are going to travel. Let's stop complaining and enjoy it. I said just that in a major newspaper, and a few thousand folks stopped to rethink the travel experience. Airports are a fact, so like the Pointer Sisters opined, let's get excited.

My story is a simple one: I like airports—mainly because no one is bugging me for answers there—and yet I'm unable to find another soul who does. So I decided to publicly see how much I could get people to stop bitching about them. I wrote a piece in the business section of the *New York Times* that displayed ways folks can love much-hated business travel.

I scribbled the story in response to watching folks get negative in a weekly column that I, like the miserable people, read every week while shaking my head. I decided that since my work was "mostly just a lot of crazy travel," mostly short-hop domestic trips at least once a week, I had a story to tell that was for the first time just full of joy.

You see, about five years ago, after nearly three decades of living in a town called New York, I moved my partner and myself to Palm Springs, California.

The only trouble is that my business is still headquartered in Gotham. And that means I have added coast-to-coast travel to my itinerary.

After trying loyalty to a single loving airline ("What? I'm not your only passenger? A pox on you!"), I switched and gave up after a gate attendant told me that I was just one frequent flyer among many. It was a brain moment: instead of caring about which airline flew me, I completely changed my mindset and started to look at my business trips as adventures or opportunities to find (maybe made-up) hidden gems in or around airports in every major American city that I could muster.

I also figured: who else gets to see America these days on company money?

Honestly, I just wanted to stay sane.

I became the gentleman who stood and chatted about local politics and scandals with the really cool sunglass saleswoman at Salt Lake City and then had a "wodka" with a great Russian bartender in Phoenix. Then in Denver it was stocking up at the Chocolate Factory, followed by Minneapolis, where I strolled along the wicked flat space up top. And Portland, where I leave the airport to see the gorgeous, lush greenery outside! Who knew that this out-of-the-way land was so full of adventure?

I told my story about leaving the airport in San Francisco—not telling my local clients I was there—and during the 90 minutes between flights commandeering a friendly cab driver and making him take me to dim sum in Chinatown. There I became a tourist in a town where I've spent thousands of hours working.

Since the story broke, I have received over 182 well-thought-out letters from people both cheering my non-woe-is-me attitude ("I don't know you," said one, "but I sure like you!") and also giving me tons of suggestions. Please come and visit them, and me, at plannedlayovers.com, one of a few clubs that cost bubkas to join. Visit me; there's no fee—not now at least.

I sure enjoyed having one or two of the e-mails tell me that the writer was going to take a brand-new look at traveling, because suddenly he or she realized that moaning about going somewhere sure made no sense.

Oh, and what's happened since? I began to pan for what appeared to be goldlike items in mountains outside Charlotte, North Carolina. And then I went to Seattle and met a radio talk show host, who had me tell my stories to his listeners. "Imagine," he said to my grin. "A guy who likes domestic business travel."

When I rode horses in Cincinnati during a stopover, the people there knew about my planned nonobsolescence from a local story in the paper (that I did not spin).

As I said then and stand by today: for out-of-airport experiences, the world needs to remember that airports are just malls and online schedules can be your pal.

By the way, to you phony "road warrior" types, I grant a hint. No one clocks as many miles as I do unless he's an international spy, and then it doesn't count. So stop your bellyaching and have a good time. Besides, ask the dude who never leaves his apartment and he will surely tell you: I *wish* I'd get out sometimes, you lucky dog.

Orgasm-Free Corporatized Sex

I am watching Gwen Stefani in her airbrushed greatness and thinking, "This is sexy?" What happened to dirt, real dirt, not the Christina Aguilera/Justin Timberlake made-for-television faux heat?

Since time immemorial, everything that is considered sticky-dirty-sexy-nasty has been picked up for sale by some corporate entity, and the No Doubt singer, "Gwen," and also the other one-named hot trotter, Black Eyed Peas' Fergie (whom I swear looks nothing like the Duchess of York), immediately creep (key word, creep) to mind. They are merely products, like an Abercrombie & Fitch model who stands still for the cameras and does what she is told. Images of what's acceptable are set by corporate entities, and I see that changing not one iota in this coming decade. Because this is how America works—and until we stop allowing the monied, religious, righteous, and so-called upstanding citizens to dictate standards, we won't do a thing about it.

I am looking at you, America. Young country, very immature about sex and sexuality. Everything makes U.S.itarians uncomfortable—which is why anything onscreen that critics deem to be "like real sex" gets so much play by a prurient corporate media.

And finally, the demonizing of sexual predators who have done their time is something that this great nation will one day have to deal with. Like anything else that took time for us to deal with *legally*, like miscegenation, homosexuality, age of consent, and that old stalwart sodomy, this immature country will one day have to realize that its call to end people's freedom after they've paid their debt to society—and are back on the so-called streets—is going to have to be reconsidered, with a deep, heavy breath.

Back to Gwen for a split second—the harsh whisperer on the radio who tells us she wishes she were "a rich girl." Is there anyone who believes that she, like Fergie of Peas or Britney or Jessica or even a real hottie like Angelina Jolie and that lit-up Jennifer Esposito, can do anything outside the boundaries of what the corporations that *pay them* will allow? Don't make me laugh. Madonna took a risk with the book *Sex* and quickly readapted to becoming a serious actress/mother/ballad-singing phony the second her label took umbrage and said so.

No rebels in this sidebar. The acceptable will out.

See Laermer.com/divas for my dissertation on the difficulty of being one-named, à la Cher or Sly, these days, what with everyone holding boring monikers like Kate or Ashley or Jennifer.

SAVVY MUSCULAR OLD PEOPLE

TREND: Old people will now be in the workplace more than ever. Get used to it. It all became clear to me in 2007 when a woman became the first baby boomer to collect social security. Pause and reflect on one crucial fact: you are going to be old one day, too.

What's the deal with old people being brought into the workplace? It's not a pretty picture. In the same way that I often hope the people who work for me will grow the heck up, and they seem to remain childish or churlish or both, we will never respect the seniors. Most of the information on our friend the Web says that older employees are less respected by, and even less able to work with, their younger (better-looking) counterparts. Technology only accentuates the differences. Old people are afraid of so much of the new that even when they are shown that "vlogging" can be done with $10 software from Radio Shack, they still don't want to participate in anything new/different.

A couple of dozen of reports I've read have cited the fundamental problem that oldsters and youngsters want different things from their jobs. It turns out that young and old feel differently about the jobs they hold: it's about sacrifice and an ability to act independently. The young won't sacrifice shit. The old will. The young don't care if they have a thousand bosses— it's only a job—whereas the old have risen in the ranks and the idea that some young whippersnapper is going to tell them what to do ain't going to cut it, Sonny.

I saw some stats about this; here goes another unplanned list (not another):

1. Workers between 45 and 54 stayed on the job twice as long as those 25 to 34, according to the Bureau of Labor Statistics in 1998.

2. Re flexibility and adaptability: the reality is that because they've seen many approaches fail in the workplace, older workers are more likely to question change. But they can accept new approaches as well as younger workers can as long as the rationale is explained.

3. The Census Bureau reports that older workers are increasingly well educated, healthier, and more likely to be female.

4. Also from the CB: "The interplay of such factors as increased education, lower fertility, delayed marriage and childbearing, and changing social norms regarding gender roles and child care has enabled many women to enter and/or return to the labor market."

Hand it to the *New York Times*, which stated with no apologies: "When older workers look for jobs, they get about as much respect as Rodney Dangerfield."

This is not to downplay the ridiculously outsized role that baby boomers play (and will continue to play) in the U.S. economy, especially compared to the young'uns. About 63 million so-called radio babies, born between 1930 and 1945 (i.e., just before the baby boom), are still in the workplace. And so are roughly 78 million baby boomers (born between 1946 and 1964; yikes, that's me). Even with large numbers of imminent retirements for these two groups, they still demographically over-whelm Generation X (48 million). By 2008, the median age of the workforce is expected to rise from 38.7 to 40.7. Contributing to these trends is the new influx of "boomerangs"—those boomer retirees who come back to the workforce after a short time away. You and me.

But the majority of the "good news" about older workers, their success, and their professional relationship with younger peers comes from overseas. Let me just say that in New Zealand and Malaysia, the older workers are really honored to be welcomed at a workplace.

Here, eh. We have old people who can't be shipped out to sea—legally. And one of these days you are going to be one of them.

Me? I'm disappearing to a land where they want my wisdom. That is, after I stockpile some.

TEENS SHALL REMAIN NARCISSISTIC

(THIS SURPRISES YOU?)

`TREND:` Teens are more narcissistic than ever before—a trend too vivid to be ignored.

A client handed me a study that said that teens were inherently more interested in doing good than their predecessors had been. She felt that a survey her firm had done proved (love that word) that young people felt that good things come if you work hard for them.

It frustratingly turned out that my dumb-ass client didn't know how to read her own company's findings. Sometimes you have to drop-kick them even when they pay on time.

Today's teens—tomorrow's adults—felt that they "deserved" those good things and didn't think it was a matter of working for them.

Uncannily, when asked if they believed in karma, the same high percentage said no.

To say you should get credit for something proves that narcissism is rampant in this generation. And so, welcome to a world in which scary adults look for a huzzah for everything they do that might be considered good.

Now, I'm all for crowing about the good work one does . . . but to make a big deal out of helping someone out seems wrong. Technology is the new frontier, and the young people of today think that they are "special people" because they are adept at giving people advice on social networking sites, according to the 2007 Narcissistic Personality Inventory 40-question survey administered to 16,475 current and recent college students.

The rule of this survey was "a positive and inflated view of the self," and the survey made it clear that almost two-thirds of the most recent sample showed a higher level of narcissism than the 1982 average (when I took it!).

So students today have trouble forming meaningful relationships, tend to be materialistic, and are prone to higher levels of infidelity, substance abuse, and violence.

Fabulous. Do you need me to say more, or are you already considering the many ways to start hiring senior citizens? See "Savvy Muscular Old People."

Thoughts about Generation Broke

This Chapter Needs No Sub

TREND: Learn who these coming "leaders" are. Have no fear—or try not to.

In 1957, The Coasters put out a song, "Charlie Brown," about the little guy who just felt like everyone was out to get him. It had the ditty "Why's Everybody Always Picking on Me?" firmly ensconced as the chorus. It was considered a silly song, but it's pretty germane to me now.

That's how I, a constantly suffering, sighing, then laughing, CEO of a veteran miniconglomerate, sometimes see these so-called Millennials that everyone is yapping about.

There's a kind of dourness to this generation that makes me think that they are being defensive about everything (yes, I'm generalizing, but aren't you relieved you don't have my heart-hardening job).

Those whom I dub Generation Broke™, most—though a few differ—always have their hand out but are not really willing to work for it. They have a few serious dilemmas within their makeup that I urgently need to bring to your attention as a service to humankind over age 29:

1. They have no money woes, whatsoever. Why should they? They pay rent and martini costs. And there's always someone out there who will cover the freight.

2. They have their parents navigating and engineering their lives—and have since day one. A pal who is president of a PR firm *swears* that three of his young employees had their parents negotiate their raises. I rest that case.

3. They don't subscribe to the so-called learning via the school of hard knocks or that other thing, making the grade, or that other thing, rising up the ladder, or that other thing, earning one's keep, or that other thing, proving value, or that other thing, starting at the bottom, or that other thing, paying one's dues! Because they don't get why—and no one who raised them has told them they're anything but fabulous. "You'll get it, don't worry, honey."

4. They do believe in oat sowing. I see them out every night—work is an afterthought for many. I think the fact that most of them aren't writers of any repute is because they're so blurry from the night before. Man, I wish I could hold my liquor that well—even back then.

5. Can I stress how funny that is? Twenty dollar gimlets every night are no problem, and yet when my assistant asked someone to go and buy a magazine, she said she only had three dollars on her. Hello.

6. They need to be told they're amazing at all times. Thus the title of this essay. If you don't, they quit. "You did not make me feel good," someone said to me earlier this year. I'm still in hysterics thinking about such earnestly felt and wrongly directed sentiments . . .

7. They are too emotional and—as a rule, because here is a recent discovery—they have not separated the professional from the personal. No one showed them how to. Or to balance a checkbook. Or to say "please." Or to . . . (I'll stop and go wash the sweat off my brow).

It is, sadly, a truism how in their short lives not a single person ever pointed out that there is a supreme difference between activity and pro-activity. Just showing up, sorry, is not good enough. I've never seen a group come to meetings en masse to simply sit there, take notes, act all interested. I firmly believe that *participation* or *facilitation* has never been explained to the new twenty-somethings, and it's probably because they spend so much time in front of monitors IM-ing people and never really talking.

Me, I loved like hell those fabulous Gen Xers with their heaving shoulders who felt they should get it now—money, prestige, power, respect! Let me explain. To me, entitlement means people will work their ass off to get something they feel is due them. They ask questions, they demand real answers, and they will get in your face if you try to hem—or haw. That's passion. Those guys and gals had balls, wow. They lived to get things done. They moved up fast because they had to (no choice, it seemed).

See, if you were 27 in 1998 you had never lived through an adult downturn, and as far as you knew all that chitchat about prior slowdowns was lore, like what my own parents said to me about "going to school in the snow" during the Stone Age. If you existed only through the good times—and they did— why not think everything was going to come to you?

Yeah, you're wondering, now wait a minute. How do I know so much, *know* being a relatively strong word? After 19 years of managing twenty-somethings, I've recently decided that this is a group that collectively works hard to get credit for a job done rapidly and, for all intents, poorly.

Members of this gen owned the world before they started out in it, and aren't we glad to know them? Every single person needs to be shown slides of those fabulous "musical chairs" we witnessed in 2000, when kids who changed jobs every few seconds for money or glory found themselves, when the bubble took a hit, so low on the totem pole that they ended up working at the Gap.

Here's a one-sheet to define the GBers for your refrigerator: they are big on eye rolling and for the most part (there are wondrous exceptions, I possess a few right now at my own firm, praise be all the Lords!) think being taught is not for them since they already know it all, gosh. They would rather work a bit, get paid a lot, hang out, dance, fall down, start again.

When I was 22, just over a million years ago, I worked with some of the toughest overseers on Earth, people who forced me to envision the big picture so while I'm flip, I'm sad.

Who will mentor people with arms so folded? Why, no one, interestingly enough. [See "Gap of Mentoring (Generation Broke™, Part Two)].

I caution you not to bother worrying about Brokers "taking over the world." No oldsters retire. They have to outsource to someone, chump! I am thrilled to take their money.

Started a bit of a tumult online when I posted a bit of this. Find responses below:

"Thank you for vindicating my own suspicions and disbelief and sadness re: the generational malaise. Disregard anything you may hear about the 'Midwestern work ethic.' It's all over the country."

"I graduated high school in 2002, and immediately enlisted in the United States Navy . . . The role-models and examples of greatness in our world have changed since Gen-X. Whereas Gen-X looked up to barons like Warren Buffett, and emulated the fictional characters of Gordon Gekko, Gen-B is left with media whores like Paris Hilton and Britney Spears."

"You hit the nail on the head, but you quit hammering too soon! Here's another trick I learned in my twenties that those today don't know—teamwork surpasses ego, especially around the office."

"Oh, how I laugh at the new grads and a few other peers . . . who expect everything on a silver platter and are not willing to bust their ass for it. I cannot tell you how many times I have stayed up until 2 in the morning working on agency/client/pro-bono/freelance work while the rest of my cohorts went out and partied."

"Generation Broke gets on *my* nerves. [As a Broker myself,] we are needy. We are greedy. And *we* don't even really know what will make us happy in our professional lives."

"When we hire a lawn service instead of insisting that our sons and daughters get out the mower, who's to blame when they roll their eyes at anything that smacks of grunt work?"

"Just like beauty is in the eye of the beholder, perhaps the ineptitude is in the tongue of the lasher. When you stop seeing us as little broken-winged baby birds and start expecting and treating us like adults, then maybe that's what we'll become."

"My generation would like to officially apologize that your elders didn't praise you enough. Please don't take it out on us by making yourself feel superior if we don't get something right the first time."

"God help us all when this book hits the shelf. If this article is indicitive [sic] of the writing in his book all Mr. Laermer offers is one thing: rancor."

They Look Like Employees

They look like employees and sound like them, but they certainly act like people who know everything. No matter what you call this group, its members arrive in the office without any ideas of their own, only those that other people tell them—all of it online and very little of it with substantial foundation.

Not *every* person aged 21 to 29 is among this group, but, well, here is the Harris Interactive Poll of 2007 to explain better than I can. When asked what they want in a job, they answered a bit too honestly. Top four desires:

- Flexible work schedule: 92 percent

- Requires creativity: 96 percent

- Allows me to have an impact on the world: 97 percent

- Want coworkers who make work fun: 90 percent.

Fun, huh?

I believe it's time (high, low, or in between) that someone stopped being so polite about the dangers inherent in this. Anyway, one day these people will rule the world. Unless, of course, people like us don't ever retire, since they may outsource everything.

That's why—oh, don't get me started.

GAP OF MENTORING (GENERATION BROKE™, PART TWO)

TREND: We'd better talk to twenty-somethings about the big picture. I know business book sales will suffer (sorry, McGraw-Hill). We don't want worker bees running the world.

As I was trying in vain to grow up, people always said that there was a generation gap between young whippersnappers like me and those ahead of me. I saw it clearly because the folks on high always had a superior look to them; I figured that was my cross to bear.

I have to hand it to those buggers: they always spent time with me on the job, walking me through the pitfalls and foibles I'd face if I wanted to take my work seriously. They took the time to point me in directions I'd never have been able to go without them.

I met an SVP type who told me he's afraid that nobody younger knows anything about what it takes to lead. He was always hoping to be better at bringing younger people up, but he just couldn't. Why? He had no time; he was worried about the job *he* was doing; too many folks (young, old, and hard-to-discern) were gunning for his job, or at least his responsibilities; and he didn't believe the comers really wanted it.

Well, they do, but they don't know how to ask because they haven't yet seen that just doing tasks over and over again will not lead to greatness. In the coming years, experts say, it is imperative that the gap be closed by forced mentoring of the twenty-somethings, and that means sitting down with them outside the 9 to 6 and saying, "This is how I do my job" or explaining how it all comes together, joining the dots that often remain disconnected.

This will pay off for both parties, who will ostensibly have a better relationship based on a little bonding that goes a long way.

WORK PERSONALITY– LIFE PERSONALITY BALANCE

IS ANY TOWN BIG ENOUGH?

TREND: We will all begin to realize that "being different" outside of work, that is, trying to be one person one hour, another during another, is an implausible waste of energy. Welcome to finding a career to match our personalities, circa 2011.

In her book *Am*Bitch*ous*, Dr. Debra Condren says that career-oriented women have to fight in order to get any work-life balance. Women, she exclaimed, are constantly fighting between maintaining their personal lives and maintaining their professional ones. Women feel that there has to be a sweet spot. You can give up on some personal goals and some professional ones, but in the end you can have it all!

Dr. Condren believes that for women there is no such thing as real balance. Achieving an apparent balance means that you're doing everything partially and nothing well. Maybe she's wrong and this is true not just for women but for every one of us who has to get up at 6 or so, slop on some soap, and drone off to work!

It's coming, though, because work personality–life personality balance is what the new decade is really about. After 10 years of struggling to figure it all out, we can have our cake and eat it too. Read on.

Picture this: the guy kisses his wife, pats his teenaged daughter on the head, chucks little Timmy under the chin and ruffles his hair, then heads off to work. At work, he spends his day being Mr. Tough Boss. He yells; he screams; he is a hard-ass who pretty much spends his day wishing he could get home a little earlier so he wouldn't have to continue being At Work Guy (AWG). He knows his employees hate him, but it's just the freaking way it has to be, and he wishes to heck they knew he was more than Mr. Tough Boss. He is desperately seeking a way to balance his work personality and his life personality, and he doesn't know how to do it because he's that guy. His career, he figures, depends upon him being him.

But there is no such thing as work personality–life personality balance. If you're maintaining any semblance of balance, it's because you're still dividing yourself between two goals—and because it is just too difficult to maintain a personality that is not your own, you'll continue to end up unhappy and frustrated. What Carl or Cindy C. had better comprehend is that by removing the pressures of "trying to achieve balance," we'll have a much clearer idea of what jobs are really right for us— what careers we should kill to move up in. No matter what, it will be about moving up, because that's the meaning of aspiration.

In the new era, our natural dispositions and personalities will point us to careers where we can feel fulfilled inside and outside of work—and act as the same person! We need to ultimately maintain the same personality in both periods of our day. Instead of trying, and ultimately failing in the attempt, to balance our lives, why not find the right position or career in which we can truly be ourselves and work to maximize our vividly appealing and obvious strengths instead of constantly trying to minimize our faults?

In the coming period that I love so much, I promise we will all begin to move away from classic positions and traditional leadership roles. Instead, folks will veer from the steady path toward positions that are more in tune with who they see themselves as being. As baby boomers leave the job and find that their only possible next step is to create their own next step, and as Generation Zero takes to the workplace with an "I'll try it for a few months, and if I don't like it, I'll take my toys and go home" attitude, you'll see more and more workers (some skilled, some not) searching endlessly for the right position at the right company.

The right position at the right company will play to people's individual strengths and allow them to work best within their personality type (and if they don't find the right position, don't expect them to stick around for long).

Change the pronoun now! It's really a matter of being you! Don't you love my use of exclamation points! So, hey, with some effort you can manage your workforce better, get higher levels of productivity, feel like yourself at work, and not pretend to be someone else. And gone will be the harried days when Carl Corporate comes home exhausted and disgusted and in desperate need of an after-work martini to help him shake off the horrors of his day. In his place will be a healthier, happier man who can be himself both in and outside of the office.

I want to know him. And you want to be him.

THE TRUTH ABOUT "KIDLESSNESS"

AND THE FUTURE OF PALS WITH A LITTLE ONE BETWEEN THEM

TREND: It's all about friends, not babies. If you're offended, take a number.

If your parents never had children, chances are you won't either.

—Dick Cavett

Remember the *Seinfeld* episode where the Long Island couple wanted Jerry and Elaine to "Come and see the ba-a-aby!"

That cry is being heard less and less because too few people are having kids, and the trend is creeping upward. A non-child-rearing population is taking over in ways that our forefathers would have been scared to see coming.

A close female friend and I have had the same running joke for years. When asked about our prospects for having children now, one of us will just chuckle: "No pets, no kids."

It's that simple.

In years to come, being kid-free will become less of a stigma—and instead elicit jealousy pangs! People with no kids get to do everything, and yeah, we get it, the child's kiss and hug is sure wondrous, and yet people wonder if the cleanup followed by terror is worth it. What fresh hell!

If you, like me, are running on the selfish track, you find it hard to imagine what it's like to be with a child, not to mention a single adult, 24 hours each day.

Here's my tale. Three of my closest lady friends had babies in their forties after swearing off the thought. They all got happiness—each of them has regrets that she shares with me only under alcohol. One of my friends actually said, "You don't like kids" to me, knowing full well that I love them. But in your home. I don't mind being insulted, but I've held strong. You tell people like me that it's "all different" with children, and I'm sure it is—in ways that can be understood when you're there.

Even oh-so-cool parents with a sitter on deck don't really live their old lives—they only pretend to unless they aren't good at being parents. A faker I know had a babysitter in his building come by at a snap so that he and the missus could stay out drinking till 2; the baby was a few months ago. It sounded like he was all about the baby possession—I mean, spending nights with the kid is a major positive of procreation!

People like me don't like any kind of guilt hanging over us, so we pass.

And friendship takes a hit as soon as kids come into being—and that is a new reason why "urbitudinal" moms are closing their wombs to kids. Witness a press release from 2007 out of the University of Florida.

> Women view childlessness much more favorably than men do, likely because parenting places greater demands on mothers, especially those juggling work and family responsibilities, a new study finds. Can you imagine this [I couldn't]: a woman takes off an average of 11 years from career for family!

So, uh, yeah. Parenthood has different consequences for women than for men, or so explained Tanya Koropeckyj-Cox, a sociologist whose study is published in *Journal of Marriage and Family.* "Although fathers have become more involved in child-care and housework in recent decades, they provide fewer hours and generally less intensive care on average than mothers," she said.

That press release said: "Results suggest that women regard both childbearing and marriage as being less central and more optional in women's lives," Koropeckyj-Cox said.

A lot of people have decided—see the following statistics—that they don't want to be the ones who mutter "You would understand if you had a child" to their pals.

Based on the U.S. census from 2003, 44 percent of women aged 15 to 44 are turning away. In 2010, that is projected to have risen to a child-free movement that has some statisticians worried. In Europe, it's been a slow buildup, and the next decade looks scary. Whereas the United States has a 2.0 fertility rate (the average number of children that a woman is expected to give birth to), Italy has for years had a 1.2. European countries are taking steps to address the specter of sharply uncompetitive workforces. Italian Labor Minister Roberto Maroni announced that the government will offer incentives to keep people at work past the minimum retirement age of 57. New workers are missing.

Spain has a doozy of a birthrate problem. According to the WHO, its fertility last year was 1.1, the lowest in Western Europe. In North America, a new study (by David Foot, demographer, University of Toronto) says that as more women are getting highly educated, they wait longer to have kids—sometimes until they no longer have the desire.

I speak—shaking my head in delight—of a politically incorrect movement, a crazy change of pace, that started around the world recently. It's called Childfree. This differentiates those who choose from those who simply cannot. One of my favorite organizations is called No Kidding! International, a nonprofit club for singles and couples who stand firm. Jerry Steinberg calls himself the Founding Non-Father, and he claims that people are starting chapters everywhere, with their own hilarious lingo, too—like *bratley* for bad kids and *PNB* for parent/not breeder, a way of acknowledging that someone did it right.

Unruly children make the kidless nuts! I've said to my friends who complain about their messy homes: "I didn't tell you to have them."

We are stating the unobvious: "I'm friends with you, not with your kid."

Yes, yes. There is a kinder and gentler side to the chapter. I turn to Lisa Groen Braner, author of *The Mother's Book of Well-Being*, who explains that something happens to parents, and new moms in particular, that makes motherhood an all-consuming experience. "Friends need to be patient, during the first year especially. The mother [and father] get sleep-deprived, she may be nursing. Her whole perception of the world is altered. And the moms need to understand that not everybody finds talking about babies all the time completely fascinating" (Beth D'Addono, "Can This Friendship Survive?" *The Star-Ledger*, August 3, 2003).

In paraphrasing an old folk song, "What shall we do with the childless?"

A few years ago I got invited to a first birthday party. I like parties, although you wouldn't have known it from the hissy fit I pulled that afternoon—for it was nightmarish. Everyone was someone who owned a kid. I demurred and ran from the room. I was the topic of conversation for the rest of the guests. As this book was being put to bed, I overheard at a salon: "I said I'm not able to make her three-year-old's party, and boy was I evil. She snapped at me—big time: 'Can't you just drop the gift off and leave?' Is that what it's come to?"

For the millions of us who choose to remain without offspring, it's our yucky freedom after all. We find it strange when people inform us what great parents we would make. And yet, we have to thank *someone* for keeping the race alive.

Found the Fnord in all this yet (Forgot already? See "Why Smart Spellers Can Spell Fnord and Why It Really Matters.")? You think I'm talking about kids, but I'm saying that friendship is what matters. If the bond is real, it survives distances, fights, kids, illness, and even death. It doesn't matter who lives in the house. You were there before, and you will be there when the nest is empty. A friendship is like a garden. You have to tend it and water it. Or the thing dies. (Yes, more Sondheim.)

Ah, to Be Nice, Perchance to Dream

TREND: It's about to be time to stop relishing all that clucking! Positive natures begin at home. And while I'm at it, I'd like to suggest that we all get a few hobbies.

As I type, I just got off my eighth flight in nine days, and everywhere I went there were citizens relishing their bad times (the national pastime). So today I'm thinking about my own interactions. It is time to stop participating in a world in which people find everything "wrong"—and are devilishly involved in the wholesale badness of everything.

What would happen if everyone stepped out of their house for, say, one whole week and gave up the art of eyerolling—I'm including me? This isn't Mr. Pollyanna speaking; it's merely an idea I got while watching U.S.-residing folks in eight different places make their lives just that much more difficult with their sour attitudes.

There was the woman online at the fake "airport Starbucks" (nothing like the local—there I am, complaining). Anyway, this lady was going on about having to stand in line, as if whatever she had to do was of consequence to anyone, meaning her too.

There was a lady sitting next to me as the pilot sweetly announced a 20-minute wait to fly off to New York (something about the U.N. and private jets and the president). She could not believe the audacity of George W. Bush holding us up!

There was this guy with two hands on two hips, enunciating his predicament to the woman at the desk as I cracked up: "I realize it's a 30-minute flight, but I do not care. I need that upgrade. I must have it."

Again, why do people make it tough to exist? Their stomach lining must hate them.

So without further misanthropy, I offer help for everyone . . . advice that sank into me while I was enduring my eight experiences.

1. Stop making it seem as if everything is "drop dead" important. We all have deadlines and bosses who ask a lot (go ahead, laugh). Yet everyone knows that this is the Age of Mediocrity, the weirdest era in which everything is just below the water level. What do I mean? Nothing is really urgent.

2. Don't play the blame game. Solutions are everywhere. Work hard to find them. You will then be surprised at how everyone relaxes when you say, "I know we'll work this out. Let me start." I tried that recently and was amazed at how everyone's shoulders relaxed and no one cared about the fuck-up that until that second had been the end of the world. It never is, meanwhile. *The end of the world is the end of the world* is the "defuser" I use.

3. Stop writing everyone with insider comments. Have you noticed a trend? Everyone wants their notes to you to be so pithy and funky, and they all have to read like *Radar* magazine or Gawker.com or some other higher-motivated-than-

thou postulator. So many e-mails I've reviewed while writing this book are heavy with jokes about "Paris" (the Heir) and "Kevin" (FedEx). Could this be another way of saying, "I have nothing to say"? Say it without the snarky asides.

Compliment more often, particularly in underwritten e-mails.

4. While I'm on the subject of subject lines, can people stop writing without *any* starter conversation whatsoever? To just barrel in is so uncool. You can remember the last time (a while ago, I'm sure) someone said, "Hey, you looked good" or "I was just thinking how terrific you are." Those stick inside. So many e-mails are all, "Here's what I want to tell you." Quid pro quo means say something nice.

5. Gossip is boring, and no one's out-of-home behavior shocks us anymore. Go ahead, point fingers and expend energy talking about the crap you're sure others have pulled; my grandma always said: "Find the positive, since it lasts longer." I realize that Tony Robbins has been extolling the virtues of good forever, but in the Age of Mediocrity, we have to think about a government that often makes us feel like losers. So perhaps we should lift each other and acknowledge the good. Those folks at these airports/ planes/bars were all about their problems of the minute. From what I could eavesdrop, they were banal.

6. More on this: it's not only about concentrating on what's worth high-fiving. When you think about it, you've got to do the same for yourself. I paraphrase my friend Sondheim from a charitable song: "Don't put yourself down. Let others do that. They usually do." For example, one of the passengers next to me was, I'm sure, a professional sighing champion (PSC). Preflight, this guy sat on the phone (naturally) and let everyone know his life was so sucky. I did my

best to ignore him. But then his pillow fell to the aisle; the passenger behind him tossed it back, kind of over him, and said it was so that people wouldn't step on it. Mr. Yucky went ballistic, and that's when I stepped in: "Relax. She was giving it back. That was courteous." He snarled. I changed my seat. Who wants to spend hours next to that? When this guy ends up institutionalized, he'll recall the pillow tossing, and sigh again.

7. Manage up. It was once felt that the tone of a company was set by management. No longer. These days, with the undeniable force of a bursting-forward generation running through offices with verve and style, it's up to the said kids to stop the drama that fills empty spaces. And why empty? It's more fun to gossip than to work, I guess. I stop the list with my final note to Generation Broke: young people need to create an example that proves that they're there to work, learn, gather comrades, get further in the world, and not be nodded toward as a bunch of drama queens.

8. Do you think I have enough lists in this book?

We all know how easy it is to criticize, to damn people, to find fault, and—like me—use endlessly flowing sarcasm as a mood enhancer. But as the planes themselves do each day, it's letting out air pollution. People who are well fed, somewhat educated, and willing to think for a living must not be the type who make any money off bad air.

And bad hair—I will say that's another story.

part nine

EPILOGUE

AND OTHER CHAPTERS I COULDN'T FIT ANYWHERE ELSE SO STUCK THEM HERE

Terms I Made Up
+ Newfangled
Future Speak

TREND: Inside references for me to share, you to bring to others, and so on.

The next 12 years will be full of mad, crazy, innovative ways of speaking to one another. And much of what we say will use terms that only you and I know. Unlike what we saw in the 1990s, where many new "verbs" were created, such as Googling, TiVoing, and Laermering (hee, hee), we are going to be moving into a private speech composed of newfangled, acceptable words that the people we talk to daily will comprehend. It's a little elitist, sue me, but there's nothing wrong with being at one with the ones you like most.

With that, I give you my list of words/terms/phrases/giggles that I want to share with the people who will be spending the most time with me, on the pages of 2011, and on the World Wide Factory at Laermer.com. See you there.

Note that many of these are coinages, because that's the way I think. You may disagree. In which case, let's start a debate on my only Wiki: websitetoolbox.com/mb/2011.

1. *Wilson* (as in "Don't Wilson me"). His name was Wilson Wilson, Jr., and he was Tim's neighbor on *Home Improvement*. Remember how you never saw anything but his eyes and maybe some nose? When someone leans over your cubicle wall and watches you, he's Wilsoning you. (See the sidebar "Feel the Verb.")

2. *Ishers.* Your friends and mine who can't stop saying *ish*. It's like nails on a blackboard.

3. *Eye rollers.* The types who are always telling you that they already know what you can teach them.

4. *Practactics.* The ideas that people come up with can be crazy as all get-out, but if they're not doable, what is the point? Practactics is the science of keeping it real.

5. *Peerspective.* How you are seen by others. Everyone needs to ask their colleagues and get some bad press every now and then. It keeps them "fresh."

6. *Bleepless.* When someone says something naughty and another says we shouldn't talk like that, and a third party stands up for the offender by saying, "Grow up. What are you? The FCC?"

7. *JetBlued.* Being stuck on the tarmac for however long. It has to be called what it's become, natch.

8. *Gmoot,* or Get Me One of Those. It's what companies say about the stuff competitors do!

9. *Committease.* The way of the world—and one that we must stop. Ideas are formed and re-formed and changed and

thought over by groups of people in the same organization. Come up with an idea, get buy-in for it, and make sure it survives.

10. *Phone karma.* Here's how it works: you call people who call people for a living. Keep that in mind. This can be used in all communication technologies, such as IM, e-mail, and networking sites. Please don't let anyone stop you from talking to him or her on the phone—if someone acts rude, shout out, "Dude! Remember phone karma!"

11. *Disruptitude.* Doing something with the right attitude that knocks people off balance. That's the way to get wooden (think bored) countrymen to react to your brand.

12. *Footnotoriety.* When someone is famous, but only in an offhanded, who-is-that kind of way. Example: Leslie H. Wexner. Super famous in Columbus, Ohio.

13. *TechnoStalgia.* The devices like old modems and one-way "drug dealer" (plumber) pagers that you keep in your attic or closet, readying to sell on eBay.

14. *Vacationot.* In the 1980s, when we couldn't get away, we took a Quaalude and vegged out for a few hours. Now we leave for one day of faux relaxation and keep in touch with everyone. It's a sad, sad situation, and it's getting more and more absurd.

15. *BlackBerry bob.* What you call it when someone is talking to you from behind a table or desk and persistently looking down at his lap. He isn't admiring his crotch.

16. *The GM nod.* People sit in a meeting together, talking about new ideas, and everyone agrees that "hitting it out of the box" is the way to go. Yes, sir, absolutely. Until everyone gets up and you hear people saying to one another: "No fucking way are we doing that." Begun in Detroit.

Finally, there is the dreaded *trendhopper*, which is the name I have for someone who raises a finger in the air and says with unbothered-about authority: "That's how I see it playing out, so there."

SELF SOMETHING OR OTHER

TREND: It's fake to self-deprecate, and in the coming years we're going to be taken to task for it.

W hat's wrong with people feeling good about themselves? In the last few years, I've watched people get a new sense of fake confidence ("artificial" is nicer) and soar to new heights. See, in the old days of generations fighting one another and oldsters telling the younger set that it had no right, you needed to earn your place.

As eighties pop goddess Neneh Cherry intoned, "Gonna go back, way back." Back then I worked for an editor Let's call her Connie, since her name was Connie. at the *New York Times* who was a little over 100 years older than me; she assigned me to my own idea of revisiting blacklisted screenwriters whose films were suddenly being widely released for the first time since the Cold War, but she ultimately killed the article. The editor said, "You write a lot about the blacklist of the 1950s, which you really can't do since you were not alive during that period."

Nowadays, younger people would never deal with such generational *mishegos*; they know more about more, and no one would ever doubt the veracity of their knowledge. They also know less about less, and so in essence they go straight to the top, even if it's only in their minds.

Which leads me to a long-awaited point: talking about yourself as a wonderful person only gets others to either think the same or call you an ass. And there is absolutely no difference between those emotions. So flaunt it. Be confident, be proud, be egotistical, be over-the-top, be yourself, be someone else; no one cares. No one's keeping score. And finally, when you say aw shucks about yourself, no one believes you.

Someone I love told me I had an insouciant air. It's probably true. I did try to put myself down in a marvelously modest, kidding sort of way "I'm just a writer," "What do I know? I just work here," "I'm really not good at that sort of thing," "Yeah, me, like I'd really know." and I ended up laughing at myself. Who was I kidding? Does this book make me look fat? Right.

I tried being self-aggrandizing and got a lot of people listening to me—not that I wasn't doing it all the time, but when you really exaggerate the points, a lot of folks wonder if perhaps you're telling the truth.

In the end, which this chapter has reached, you have to be larger than life to make a point! It's noisy. Haven't I said that? Are you not listening?

I know better—at least better than you. Let me tell you a story.

GOOD MORNING, TODAY IS JANUARY 21, 2011 . . .

TREND: In 2011, the 2006 era will be seen as a long time ago. Let's imagine . . .

Five years ago it was the start of 2006, a year that transported us into a different era.

In 2006, a number of issues on the national security agenda fueled an ongoing debate concerning executive privilege. In the first 5½ years of his presidency, George W. Bush signed more than 1,100 bills and vetoed one on stem cells. But the president issued "signing statements" signaling that he was not going to comply with about 800 provisions included in about 100 laws—more challenges than all previous presidents combined.

Guantánamo and black sites. President Bush announced that 14 high-level al-Qaeda prisoners had been transferred to the Guantánamo prison camp from secret CIA "black sites" around the world. It was the president's first official acknowledgment of extraordinary "rendition," or transferring of suspected terrorists to detention centers in foreign countries where U.S. laws do not apply and detainees can be subjected to "alternative interrogation procedures." Along with Abu Ghraib, Guantánamo has become a political liability for the administration, a symbol for many of an inhumane and ineffective strategy in combating terrorism.

Corruption scandals. Powerful Republican lobbyist Jack Abramoff was convicted of fraud, tax evasion, and conspiracy to bribe public officials. He agreed to testify against politicians and former colleagues in a wide-ranging corruption investigation. Abramoff had collected millions in fees in exchange for congressional support of legislation benefiting his clients, which included Indian gambling casinos and sweatshops in the Marianas Islands. Former House majority leader Tom DeLay (R-Tex.) resigned because of improper fundraising and the taint of his long association with Abramoff; two of DeLay's aides were convicted in connection with the scandals.

Immigration reform. In nationwide demonstrations in April and May, more than a million immigrants, primarily Hispanic, staged marches in more than 100 cities. Protestors called for immigration reform, which included allowing America's 11 million undocumented workers the opportunity to work legally. Many of the protestors had been mobilized by a December 2005 House bill, since stalled, that would have turned illegal aliens into felons, ineligible for any status (lack of documentation constitutes a violation of civil, not criminal, law).

Midterm elections. The November midterm elections led to a shift, with the Democrats gaining control for the first time in 12 years.

And the Iraq War. Polls throughout 2006 indicated that the issue of greatest concern among Americans was the ongoing war in Iraq. Spiraling Sunni-Shiite violence and the diminishing hope that some of the roughly 140,000 U.S. troops would be able to withdraw before the end of the year led to a uniquely low approval rating for President Bush.

In 2007, when this book was being put to bed, harkening back to 2002 seemed like a million light-years ago! When I think about that period, it's a wholly distinct era from "now": examples are the beginning of the rebuilding of Ground Zero, spinach deaths, the hobbled economy, the death of the Queen Mother, WorldCom becoming the latest disgrace, the bombing of Bali, the Catholic Church scandal at its height, and a pretzel *doing in* a president of the United States.

> That's what the future does: recolors what was super bright light just a couple of years ago.

Contrarianism Is Next to Godliness

Some points to consider when you have a moment:

1. One night, the City of Miami recently made most of its stores stay open all night, and the cash registers never stopped ringing. I often wonder when the 24-hour party mentality will take over this country—it's already starting. In New York, a Korean hairdresser hilariously called Hair Party 24hr just opened on the east side. (This is very big in Seoul, we are told.) For anyone who has lived in New York

of late, you know what I mean when I say: "This city tends to sleep." It's time to keep places open—it's a chicken-and-egg situation, and the chicks will roost if you offer them a home. Finally, when will the airlines fight for the right to use the empty skies in the middle of the night? Seems like it would solve a huge problem for overextended fliers, or is logic not part of the equation?

2. It's not such a small world, after all. Every week someone tells me he or she ran into someone and isn't it amazing, we hardly realized the connection, etc., etc. That's hogwash. We are a classist society—we run with the same type of people, and so inevitably you'll be sitting next to someone in a theme park ride who went to school with someone you nearly killed while dating. Or you will find out that someone intimately knows someone that you intimately know. I really hope that as a society we can just give up the Disneyfied notion that we all come together eventually—it's not happening. We all just tend to run in the same circles.

3. Every single time a product says that it is not marketing to consumers, but rather is "targeting the enterprise"—the business end of the market—watch for the turnabout. All the PDA companies told me they would never target the people when I asked them for my first trend book—but after the Palm succeeded royally, each one enacted huge all-out pushes to focus on the "prosumer" (that is, consumers who happen to be professionals). Sounds like jargon in order to reach the same goal: anyone who works for a living who reads *Us* magazine.

4. After 100 years of hearing dramatic protesting too much, we won't fall for the "I am retiring" jam that stars have employed to get our attention. It's not merely the likes of Barbra Streisand, Cher, the Who, Tina Turner, Jackie Mason (just opened March 2008, in what he bills as his "final New York performance"), or even the Eagles, who cheekily named a 1990s live reunion "Hell Freezes Over." And gosh, some film types enact the campaign without shame: interchangeable actor Hugh Grant quit the business loudly a few years back, and film/TV/theater/wig director Mike Nichols announced his leave. Both quickly forgot.

   Actually, what killed this ploy was when those who, unlike Genesis (who called theirs "The Final Tour?" hilariously), didn't need to announce the end, like Jay-Z, played us. Z's Fade to Black tour, album, movie, site, and bubble gum cards were fake, needless, foolish, and silly, since he didn't need to garner the love, and instead fan patience ran thin. Witness how awfully his "comeback" did two years later when, perhaps his best CD ever, *American Gangster*, dropped and stayed dropped.

5. No one would believe it at a party recently, but I found a movement that actually decries eating anything that isn't found! You've heard me say how people would be happier if they had hobbies—well I'm unsure if this group has one or needs a saner suggestion (Freegan.info).

6. Straighten Up and Fly Lite: At first blush, it's a smack-your-forehead I can't believe this hasn't been done before thunderbolt. FlyLite: a remote wardrobe manager for frequent flyers. Simply, it holds clothes and items with which you regularly travel. You pick and choose what you want on a trip. And when you arrive—there's everything you need. Delivered clean and ready to go. When you leave, everything's stored until—whenever. Physical and psychological relief for harried travelers who need it the most and are most able to pay. It's an obvious inspired extension of our "on demand" culture, so you get almost anything—from HBO to snow tires—just snap your fingers (use jazz hands, ¿ sí ?)! No more last-minute laundry, no more suitcases to suit up with, no more luggage to lug. Fewer hassles at check-in, no carousel crowds, lower airport stress all around. Sure thing, right, Cusack?

   Well, no. We just know that FlyLite ain't gonna fly. Yes, the right pieces all seem to be in place, and everything looks good on paper. But even when we see something like FlyLite—should be so simple, so successful, so natural "Will you be checking any luggage to Detroit?" "No, I'm FlyLiting." we can't help but be skeptical to a fault. It's a shame, but it's killing plenty of good ideas before they make hay.

   Problem is: we've become intractably cynical consumers. And we're especially jaded when it comes to any company or service or person claiming to simplify our lives. Maybe it's because every gadgeteer promising freedom becomes just another source of aggravation; everything we do takes negotiation, fellas and gals. It's also because we've been burned one time too many by service industries whose growth is matched only by their incompetence. Outsourcing of call centers, stagnant minimum wage, abandonment of the "customer is always right," which I wholeheartedly live by (the abandonment, that is), and a dozen other factums have contributed to decline of quality customer service in America.

Something has changed. We've come to expect garbage. We anticipate surliness, dysfunction, and an assured lack of accountability. Which is why, and now I'll exhale, that despite best intentions, FlyLite will never convince me, the flight-wearied businessman, that my suit will for sure definitely make it to Atlanta ahead of me.

7. The restaurant trade associations will flame me, but heck: Why does every get-together have to be over a meal, a coffee, a piece of cake, a drink? Why can't people just sit down at a desk or a couch or a tree and have a talk? Turn off the crack machines. Share thoughts. Gossip. Don't eat, and please have no waiter interrupt you just as you're about to give up a really juicy morsel of fact.

Talking is what we do to fill the soul. Eating is what we do to fill the boredom. It's simple math. "The distributive property comes into play when an expression involves both." Something like that.

Anyway, for more likeminded, yet notoriously contrarian views of the world, you know what to do: dial up Laermer.com/blogbabyblog.

You Hate This Book Because . . .

After 10½ books, I am reminded of those whom lyricist Alan Jay Lerner called "the little shits," people who have to say something bad or they won't feel like they exist.

(After reading some wild-ass things said about me, I figure lots of people will want to smash my new efforts in the mouth; in an effort to be ultimately helpful, I'll do it first.

Simply choose from the following:

- That Laermer guy cracks himself up way too much.

- I read it. It's all so random. (Wake up. Life is random!)

- How can you tell the future from the present?

- Why should I care about J. Lo, and exactly *how* will she or Jake Gyllenhaal—or Hollywood—tell me what's coming?

- I tell you, sidebars kill me. He puts in too many topics for a single tome.

- How much stuff can be in a single volume? I mean, should this be two or maybe four?

- He's like the Matsu K of books. You watch him wind up, and he just doesn't quite hit the plate—though you can *hear* him trying.

- If I hear "being well informed makes you a trendspotter" one more time, I'll kick that bastard.

- Why isn't he as self-serious about the future as Faith is? She at least makes me feel like I have to resteer the ship that's my life.

- Sidebar, shmidebar! I can't tell the difference between them and his chapters—such teeny topics. I wouldn't be a good Jew if I didn't add the old Catskills line about food served: "Oy, was it horrible— and the worst part was, there wasn't enough of it."

- Now, what is it about pop culture experts that they think they can show us how to make money? Gees!

- Is sex the root of our issues or, as Freud pondered, is it the way our mom treated us as kids?

- The Laermer machine talks and ponders and muses and finally mocks—can't anyone do that?

- He thinks social networking is a fad? Tell that to every corporation in the world. Bah.

- What's with all the lists?

- If I want to envision the future, I'll dream it. Who is Frank Pretzel?

  For more criticism—I do *everything* for you—go to FrankPretzel.com.

Final chapter before Last Words—naturally, mine:

TOP SEVEN MISTAKES SMALL BUSINESSES MAKE

A GUIDE TO SAYING WTF

TREND: Let's envision businesses knowing how to sidestep the big pothole.

During the last mercurial business cycle, I sneakily asked supersuccessful types such as Mark Cuban (Mavericks dancer), Peter Guber (Guber), David Brancaccio (*now* man on PBS), Bob Davis (Speedy Lycos dude), and Gerald Storch (Toys

"R" Us head) what killed businesses. If we can all live without these booboos, these next years will rock.

1. *Stagnation.* You've got to evolve or die. Change with the times only if you want to stay ahead of your competition. Imagine you're okay, and surely you are asleep.

2. *Lack of planning.* Find your niche, craft a plan, and then stick with it each day. Use it like a manifesto—because that's what it should be. It's easy for small business owners to get distracted and not stay focused on what they do best. If your plan isn't gosh-darn-it working, tweak quickly.

3. *Turning off loyal customers.* Too many businesses focus on bringing in new customers and ignore their loyal customers. Since 20 percent of customers are responsible for 80 percent of business, that math means it's a lot easier to keep old customers happy than to find new ones.

If your customers adore you, they'll tell everyone anyway—because they're not used to such consistency.

4. *Thinking you know it all.* If you're not thumbing through business magazines on a regular basis, checking out industry blogs and those know-it-alls who are truly influential (and often in their pajamas), and staying informed about the world, you'll be left behind, sadly.

5. *Not keeping up with your customers.* Follow trends in the media, pay attention to what businesses down the street are doing, and be a noncliché spotter of trends so that you don't become obsolete or, worse, stale. Ask customers what's working, what's not, and why. Do it without any cynicism or thin-skinned defensiveness! What's that? It means just take the criticism.

6. *Staying quiet.* Get the word out about who you are and what you offer—and don't worry about giving away the "company secrets." People should know what you're doing. Don't be self-important. Leverage marketing, Internet, and the freaking Yellow Pages, and use that ole PR for exposure: maximum style.

7. *Having a tepid message.* Think about how you want customers to feel and what you want them to do with that feeling. Then craft memorable messages—through the Web site, ads, newsletters (with real content), and face to face—messages that are bent on surprising them and that make them go "woo!"

8. I said seven—I lie sometimes. *Being inconsistent.* If you act like an asshole in public, it's probably best to give the paying customers what they want. If you're a sweetheart, show that side of you all the time. Businesses are about people—but only the ones who pay to see the fake you. That's why whenever he's on the street, the French maître d' always says, "Sorry, bub. The accent's only for paying customers." Us.

9. *Neglecting WTF.* Sometimes you do have to throw away regular old wisdom slammed down on from on high. In the face of all business odds, the bets are off—'cause who knows what you're capable of but you? Go with your gut. Ask my friend who owns an ice cream parlor in an off-the-beaten-path neighborhood in Queens. One day he decided that he just had to say what the fuck and started hawking his odd-duck flavors to hifalutin shops in major snob cities, even though the competition is a killer. Guess what? He persisted in the face of odds that would kill the normal corporate shnook, and he's on his way to becoming an icey mogul.

10. *Worrying about what people think—as if they really pay attention to you.* The biggest successes are those who enjoy being laughed at all the time. I'm the one who said that, yup. (That's all 10 now. I'm really finished.)

THE OUTRO

AN EPILOGUE COMPRISING LAST WORDS, FIRST WORDS, WORDINESS . . .

TREND: Now and then Laermer stops talking.

I wanted to write a book that would help people look ahead to the future, to do more than just get predictions about where we might be headed, and to ultimately shake off the common wisdom that prevails and fails us.

Yet this needed to be more than just a plethora of essays from me, combined with quotes and data from others with the same ostensible goal. So the only way to make this unstatic is to tell you to close this book and do what any self-respecting trend guy or gal should do: go online.

On Laermer.com you will obtain more on what's been brought up in the past 293 pages. Click on the URL after you review what I just told you; take a simple quiz. Do it once. As soon as you answer a bunch right, you are given a password for free entry. For the rest of you: pay me, bitch! It will be updated three times per week. That's a future promise from me.

This destination extraordinaire will have all over—essays, trend advice, ways to spot, a few harsh realities, my scorecard on what's right and wrong, blog posts all the livelong day, and guests that know when to leave. Laermer.com will teach you—and me—life elements to keep us up to date, such as how to

Welcome to a Business Book
for the Next Decade.

2011

TRENDSPOTTING
FOR THE
NEXT DECADE

WWW.LAERMER.COM

So that's what 2011
is: an exploration of
trends to affect our
lives and a sense of
what we have to
overcome just before
we leap into the new
about-to-be-filled
space.

GET THE
GOOD STUFF!

write cursive letters, or how to curse someone out politely! Finally, I mean it, the last words in a book you got to put down.

Have a good decade.

Notes to Part Three

76 "According to a German study . . .": J. Born et al., "Sleep Inspires Insight," *Nature*, 427: 352-355, January 22, 2004.

"And a Harvard Medical School study . . .": Robert Stickgold and Matthew Walker, "To Sleep, Perchance to Gain Creative Insight?" *Trends in Cognitive Sciences*, 8(no. 5), May 2004.

77 "Some sleepy-time devices . . .": www.new-mind.com.

"More important, Tononi was quoted . . .": Dave Tenenbaum, "Study Puts Us One Step Closer to Understanding the Function of Sleep," University of Wisconsin–Madison news site, www.news.wisc.edu/13733, April 30, 2007.

INDEX

Richard Laermer: Media Guy

Laermer is an oft-quoted source to the media and other influential types on topics regarding the future of this crazed world. Some background: the CEO of RLM PR, one of the only independent PR firms that's actually fun to work with, he is the best-selling author of *Punk Marketing*, in addition to the perennial PR handbook *Full Frontal PR* and 2002's *TrendSpotting* (plus others). He is widely sought after as a speaker and media trainer, has cohosted TLC's cult TV show *Taking Care of Business*, and has a following as a commentator for Public Radio's *Marketplace* program. His BadPitchBlog (BadRelease.com), with Kevin Dugan, is the industry's watchdog and a recipient of PRSA's Bronze Anvil Medal for Best Blog. He is the man behind Unspun Radio, available on iTunes and celestial radio stations!

Previously a journalist for many years, his work has been featured in the *New York Times*, *New York Daily News*, Reuters, *USA Today*, *New York* magazine, *Saturday Review*, *US Weekly*, *Interview*, *Crains NY*, *New York Post*, *Chief Executive*, *Soho Weekly News*, *Editor & Publisher*, and many others (all over the journalism map).

The media guy's outlandish, though logical, speeches about trends, media, and marketing have wowed audiences and intimate groups as he hosts seminars and keynotes for corporate and civic organizations, marketing groups, PR and sales forces, and genial gatherings. He resides in the City of New York—and has since birth—but is a part-time resident of La Quinta, CA. His hobbies include judging a book by its cover, studying about the future, and rewriting his bio.

Sign up at nosnoozeletter@Laermer.com to receive Laermer's ridiculously useful newsletter. You will not want the time back!

ACKNOWLEDGMENTS

I thank the people who helped to make this happen—
or supported it somehow:

Scott J. Milne

Herb Schaffner

Jeremy Katz

Erin Mitchell

Daniel Jacobson

James Lisk

David Brancaccio

Lorissa Shepstone

Ruth Mannino

Mark Ramsey

Nadia Cornier

Mark Simmons

Joe Bergeron

Sharon Nieuwenhuis

Lou and Gloria Laermer

Steve Bradley: The LOML!

witcher The Zips Bandwagoning Neo Laziness

scordianism Fnord Intrigesting Spc

ero Mr. Yucky Self Something Or Other Prosume

cing Paper Battery Anonymities Death In Be

ziness Green Fakes Caboodle Glorious B

Spoutables Disruptitude Footnotoriety La

erism SpontaNoEity Unspun YouTu

The Tens Chapterization Yada (Yada) B

s Busting Practactics Peerspective Couch-Ju

ty Laermered TechnoStalgia Vacationot

un YouTubing Postponation Wordsw

a) Baiter & Switcher The Zips Bandv

h-Jumping Zadora Discordianism Fnord Sp

ero Mr. Yucky Self Something Or Other Prosun

cing Paper Battery Anonymities Death In Be

ziness Green Fakes Caboodle Glorious E

Spoutables Disruptitude Footnotoriety La

erism SpontaNoEity Unspun YouTu